Sound of
Adventure

Kay Blevins

2013

The Sound of Adventure

This book will also appear in a large-print version.

Edited by Kelly Ferjutz

How did a big-city girl become a Powder Puff Racing competitor? Kay Blevins had lots of sheer determination and grit that wouldn't quit! It was love at first sound – the day she first heard the engine of '619, and in all the years since then, she's never forgotten it! For all of today's young girls, who think it's always been their world, here's a true story about a woman who wouldn't take 'no' for an answer—and made the skies hers! Wife, mother, business-woman, entrepreneur, Kay Blevins set her sights on a goal, and never looked back. Here is the tale of how her dream came true, along with some of the adventures that followed.

Dear Reader –

Pictures taken when flying during a race are seldom great photographs because of the Plexiglas used for windows. Reflections, the movement of the aircraft and the fact that one is dealing with vibrations can and usually does affect the outcome. Also there is only time to take them when things are quiet and the photos one really would like during the bad stuff are never possible because we are way too busy staying up! Also the turbulence creates its own difficulties. So we apologize, not only for that, but also, many of the slides we scanned for this book were more than thirty or so years old and had not been stored in a climate-controlled environment. The quality deteriorated somewhat, but they tell a story when mere words cannot begin to do justice to the scene.

Kay Blevins

Dedication

Leora Lucas "Brooks" Richards

Brooks : Airline Pilot, Charter Pilot, Air Racer
February 6, 2011

To my forever friend, Brooks. I lost you today. You have always been Angel Girl, able to leap tall buildings, could smoke 'em when you felt like it, and best of all you were the sharer of the impossible dream. Soul sister, flying cohort, shaman, lovely special friend. I feel honored with my memories of you, and you will always be with me. A smile, a laugh, and you are there. Thousands of pictures of our racing together - such treasures! So fitting that your loving family added to your obituary: "Oh, I have slipped the surly bonds of earth and danced the skies on laughter-silvered wings... Put out my hand, and touched the face of God."

I am quite certain that you are busy teaching the angels to fly.

Prologue

It was love at first sound, on that gray, cloudy day at the airport in Louisville. I wasn't expecting such a thing to happen, but I knew it immediately! At first I could only hear her distinctive voice, but when the fog lifted enough that I could see her? I was totally lost.

It was in January of 1976, and my love of flying had led me to a wonderful job at the Cessna dealer in Louisville. '619 came to me new from the factory. In fact she had been on her way with two others from Wichita to Cleveland when the three of them were stopped by the weather and ended up on the ramp of the dealership. In addition to falling in love at first sound and sight, it also happened that I was in need of a plane for the 1976 Powder Puff Derby.

Sounds simple doesn't it? But when she arrived, I was getting ready to take the flight test for my commercial ticket and I had to pass that first, in order to apply to the race committee. And then too, of course, there was another *really huge* obstacle. '619 was a state-of-the-art new model (as new as a Cessna could be) with the latest in radios and equipment and she did not come cheap. In fact, the price tag was more than we had paid for our house. In fact, more than several houses.

In the background of most everyone's life there is a sound heard universally, even if not often: a growling, rumbly roar coming from the sky. But of course, that is only if it is not the whine and shriek of a jet engine. There are not many skies airplanes do not traverse and they carry with them a unique identity.

Consider, for instance, a NASCAR race. If you turn the sound off on the TV, you have missed an essential element in the identity of the race. They are just cars going around in a circle, but with sound? It is totally awesome for those who enjoy auto racing. Sound is something that triggers our attention. Focuses it, actually.

The loudness of an airplane's roar depends mostly on the engine and the plane's altitude, but to all pilots, current or not, it has the pull of the siren's call. Once you connect to a particular plane, that plane's sound is embedded into your soul's blood essence forever. Anytime we find ourselves outside when there is also a plane's passage, we usually have our head up craning to pick out the approach, all the while mentally cataloguing type, model and engine that we think it might be. Certain planes, those we have owned or flown a lot, bring special warmth to the solar plexus and a smile to our face. It is a personal thing, and experience seems to vary from pilot to pilot.

Of all the planes I have flown, plus the four that we owned from time to time, there is one special sound, whether it was idling or full throttle in a race that created such a flood of emotions I never knew whether to cry or shout for joy. The sad thing is that I most likely will never hear *my* particular heart sound again.

At least I do know she is alive, flying and teaching

others that a plane is truly not just an inanimate object. Not only is it a fully functional (almost) living, breathing, machine but it is sympathetic, empathetic and can be called upon to do the most amazing feats, all of which are unlisted in the service manual. For me, that Cessna airplane, officially titled N80619, knew exactly when and where extraordinary ability was required, and she knew it way before I did. Always. And she never let me down.

The first planes that a student flies are usually school owned, battered and bruised trainers that maybe were once someone's personal dream. But in time they grew old, and sad though it might be, were relegated to the end of the road, which is training students. Mostly only a factory-sponsored new dealership had new trainers, and that was a really rare occurrence. That isn't all bad because you learn early on in your flying career to handle a lot of emergency situations while still having an instructor to help sort it all out, because once you solo, the same things will scare you silly, but at least you just might remember what to do.

Chapter One

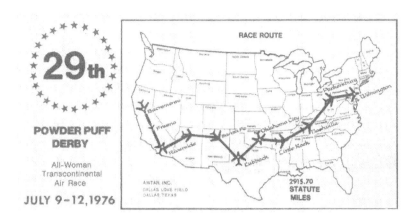

29th

POWDER PUFF DERBY

All-Woman Transcontinental Air Race

JULY 9-12, 1976

RACE ROUTE

AWTAR INC.
DALLAS LOVE FIELD
DALLAS TEXAS

2915.70 STATUTE MILES

1976 All-Woman Transcontinental Air Race
Powder Puff Derby

THE PERFECT DAY

Where does a dream begin? The elusive wisp of
an idea that gathers energy, and like a rolling stone,
creates its own momentum, a thought that sometimes
comes to nothing but at other times changes our life
forever.

Life has magical moments for all of us, but no one
can ever take my perfect day from me or change or
diminish it. For as long as I live with a sound mind I
can replay the day, the time, the sequence, the full
event in clear and living color. I can breathe the crisp
Kentucky air, I can feel the unbelievable joy of being
at one with the aircraft, I hear the wind outside, the
engine growl, the thrumming running through my feet
telling me the plane is alive, and I KNOW once again

how very lucky I am. For my perfect day was the very best of the best.

Questioning where my dream began I am aware it did not begin with someone else and their dream. No one in my family ever said they wanted to fly. No, but they did say it probably wasn't possible for me to become a pilot. There was nothing wrong with me that would be a huge challenge to overcome, other than the lack of money. I don't remember the pep talk that most parents give their children about being able to be anything they want to be and maybe they did say it, even if not very convincingly, but I knew in my mind it was a rather stupid idea. My heart told a different story.

My life changing dream to become a pilot started on a small hilltop covered in sparse grass with half a dozen small horses roaming around me. I would spend hours lying on my back being tickled by the weeds and insects just to watch the next plane enter the pattern for Pontiac Airport. I am sure it looked like a very lonely existence for a young girl but I was happy.

When I was growing up we spent every summer at a deep and cold spring fed lake in a very small cottage my family had built in 1942. Winters we were in the city near the Chrysler Plant where my father worked while I went to school, but in summer he commuted on weekends to the only place, the lake, that I ever saw him really happy. Although I had an older brother the age difference was too great for him to want to be with me, and the only other kids around were boys near his age. I endured the nickname of Tag-a-long during all of my growing up years, even

5

though I wasn't allowed to do that all too often. This could possibly be because I would beat them any chance I got whether it was in a canoe, racing to the swim raft or even in firing the rifles at practice targets.

The hill that seemed to always beckon me was about an hour's walk away from the cottage as I had to walk completely around one end of the long lake. Sometimes I would get up early and take the canoe before my brother woke and paddle as far into the reeds below the hill as I could go before clambering out to walk in the icky seaweed and muck to the shore. Disturbing the red-winged blackbirds nesting in the reeds I would hike to the top of the hill while checking for the hated bloodsuckers that lived in the marshy decayed vegetation.

Those were the days I'd grab an apple or even make a sandwich so I could stay out for as long as I wished, hating the idea of having to leave to go back home. And I would spend the day waiting for the tell-tale sound of an engine in order to crane my head when they were slightly off course to see the pilot in the cockpit. It was always a thrill to me to wonder what it was like being up there. I created different scenarios about where the plane had been and where it was headed, and thought how glorious it would feel to be up in that plane seeing everything for miles around. The dream was ignited by my imaginative mind and I discovered I was determined to see it all for myself someday.

By the time I was allowed to drive a car I had been in Civil Air Patrol for several years and had worked hard to compete for a flight scholarship. Finally the day came I had the certificate in my hands and could begin the real process of becoming a pilot. I remember the day I soloed thinking how ironic it was, as I approached that first landing, that I flew over the hill where I had stationed myself as a child and couldn't help but wonder if someone else was watching me this time around. Of course, the view from the cockpit was just as breathtaking as I always knew it would be, the world below in miniature filled with wondrous color, but the greatest feeling in every fiber of my being was of being so free.

As a Cadet I tried out for many other activities and awards which meant I attended many screenings put on by the Senior personnel to test knowledge and skill. The waiting for your turn to go before the screening board was an anxiety-filled, nail-biting time but usually the Senior waiting with you would try and put you at ease and talk about your experiences. Many of them would allow you to ask them questions, too. It was during the competition for International Cadet Exchange that I drew a female Colonel from Wing Staff to sit with me.

Finally, I could ask the question I had most wanted to ask another feminine person who had done all the things I thought I wanted to do. My question burst out of me! "What was the most exciting thing you have ever done in aviation?" Her answer was seared into my heart as she responded with not a moment of hesitation that it had been to fly a Powder Puff Derby Air Race. I knew Amelia Earhart had flown that race many years earlier.

It was over twenty years later that those words came back to me with all the emotion of that day so long ago. I had been married to my handsome cadet more than twenty years and been involved in aviation in some way all that time, frequently working at airports where I was happiest, or with Civil Air Patrol trying to repay all the dreams that had come true for me.

This particular night late in December, I had attended a *Ninety-Nine* meeting, an association made up of women pilots: this chapter meeting had been in Frankfort, KY, about an hour from home. I heard them announce that the last Powder Puff Derby would be flown that year. It rocked me so that tears streamed down my cheeks during the whole trip home and when I arrived my husband saw my face and thought I must have had an accident. I could hardly get out the words what with my wailing and blubbering that it was going to be the very last Powder Puff *–ever!!–* and I wasn't qualified to fly in it! I had achieved my dream of flying but had never acquired my commercial ticket, thinking it was somehow akin to overkill. Yet now it was a prerequisite to be able to fly in the race and there was hardly any time left to accomplish it.

Being the sweet man that he is, my husband set about looking for ways to alleviate my suffering and told me to look into what it would take. I knew it would take passing the written test and flying almost a hundred more training hours in just about 35 days. Of course a plane would be required and we had just sold our small one, which wouldn't have been accepted anyway, but to be in the drawing on Valentine's Day for a race number, the paper work had to be in with all the fees and a plane available before the fourteenth of February.

Some things had not changed much since I was a child. There just wasn't enough money to make my second dream an easy reality, but once again I embarked on the journey of checking off the lists in preparation, and I studied constantly and flew the wheel pants off the rental airplanes. Working at the flight desk of the fixed base operation at the Kentucky Flying Service at Bowman airport in Louisville was a blessing because I could schedule plane and instructor time easily but I couldn't schedule the notoriously bad Louisville weather in January. No one believed I would have enough good weather time to get ready for my commercial check ride.

Like a good fairy tale, the impossible was accomplished, I passed the written exam on the first try, and by being at the airport at all hours, I had also accumulated the necessary hours of flying needed. Now I was ready to take the flight portion of the flight exam. I was required to fly first with the chief flight instructor to be sure I was ready for the FAA examiner, so I scheduled the check flight with the desire to get it over and done with as quickly as possible. And then, I could get on to the real deal with the hard-as-nails FAA examiner, the next-to-last hurdle to cross.

The day dawned bright and beautiful and as lovely as the best Kentucky has to offer and I was so full of happiness to have made it so far. I know my exuberance was almost a put-off to the instructor as I was supposed to be taking it all very seriously, which I really was. But I was also somehow in the flow.

Thus began the perfect day. I could do no wrong. Easily, with a sharp precision that was almost unbelievable, I executed maneuvers that had been difficult only days prior. My short field landing was so short even the control tower made an appreciative comment and I was able to repeat anything a second time with the same accuracy. I thought my heart would burst with the sheer joy of it. No stumbles, no being unsure of anything even for a moment, no need for correction of any kind. The instructor was all business and made little comment, just peppered me with instruction to see if he could unsettle me. Finally the flight was over and yet I was felt like I was still flying.

As the instructor did the paperwork on the fuselage of the plane, I stood next to him, and then he said very seriously and looking straight into my eyes, "I must tell you that you will never, ever again, fly that well in the whole of your career. Don't keep looking for it to happen because it never will. Since I am also an FAA examiner I consider it unnecessary for you to fly tomorrow with the scheduled FAA examiner and I am passing you right now on your Commercial Flight Test."

Wow! It had actually been accomplished! In years to come I discovered he was right in that while there were many great days to follow, that perfect day was never again to be repeated.

Now, the moment had arrived when I had the precious temporary slip in hand, certifying I was a commercial pilot, so I could officially submit my name into the drawing for the race. Being totally focused on getting my application in on time, I went to find Dick, the owner of the flying service where I worked to talk about my dream. He was off on a charter trip and wouldn't be back until midnight. I had to go home and fix dinner so I took my pretty little temporary slip and a one dollar bill, and attached them to the note I left on Dick's front car seat. It read, "Dear Dick, I passed my check ride, and here is a dollar down on N80619. I will see you in the morning."

Then I had to go home and face my husband and tell him what I had done. He had previously thought that if by some miracle I was able to pass the flight test in time to apply, we would somehow beg, borrow or buy an old plane so I could make the race, and then sell it after the competition had ended, but that was about the extent of such thoughts. It was an interesting evening at the Blevins's household.

At seven in the morning we walked into Dick's office and unable to discern anything by what was on that poker face of his, I said we came to talk about N80619. He motioned us to sit and said, "Funny thing. I got a call from the Cleveland Zone manager this morning saying he was sending three ferry pilots down to pick up the planes." My heart dropped into my shoes.

Then he said, "And I told him only send two". My spirits started to soar. "Yes," he said, "I have a dollar down on N80619".

The Cleveland manager, after a great long silence, apparently said with strong disbelief, "Dick, I am sending three pilots down to pick up those airplanes."

And again, Dick repeated. "Only send two. I have a dollar down on the one."

Dick related that the manager then said, "Now, Dick. You are telling me you took a dollar down on an airplane that expensive? How do you think that is going to turn out?"

"Oh I reckon she'll be along in a little while and we'll figure it all out." And somehow we did. Paul was still of a mind that we would sell it when we returned, even though it had been raced and now would have a lot of hours on it so it might be more difficult. It was not readily apparent to anyone else at the time but that plane wasn't going to be sold, not for a very long time. Not until we had flown many races and had a gazillion adventures. I was in love with that plane so she wasn't going anywhere – except with me.

New proud owners, Kay and Paul, of N80619

When I had asked Laura, our nineteen-year-old daughter, then attending an aviation program at Western Michigan, if she wanted to fly with me on the very last Powder Puff Derby, the one made famous by Amelia Earhart, she said, "Sure, what does it take?" What it took was for both of us to get our commercial tickets, which included passing one really tough written and about another hundred hours of instruction and flying, all to have our paperwork in by February 14. No wonder Paul had thought it would be a miracle if we made it in time. It was, indeed. But we did it!

The weather in Kentucky and Michigan in January and February is notoriously bad for flying. Some days I would arrive at seven in the morning but have to wait for VFR, which is three miles visibility, until noon, and then flying every available hour, with instructor some of the time and solo the rest until too dark, except of course, for the required night time flying.

It was wild from beginning to end, but since Laura and I had talked my instructor, Brooks Richards, into getting a plane and flying the race also, she was invested in getting me ready, too. She had been awarded Flight Instructor of the Year for Kentucky the year before so someone was willing to loan her a plane and even funded some of her expenses, but she too had to wait for the luck of the draw after submitting the applications.

While there were to be two hundred planes selected to be in the race, there were many, many more applicants. They all wanted to fly from Sacramento, CA, to Wilmington, DE, but only a small percentage had never flown a race before. We were lucky; both

13

planes were awarded a race number and were scheduled to fly. Laura's and mine was #112. At that point, not having much disposable income, we also had to figure out how to pay the costs; not only fuel, food and lodging, but banquets, team uniforms and maps. Lots of maps!

The race route was designed to test the pilot's skill and anyone who depended solely on navigational aids would not be flying the fastest route. There was no such thing as GPS in 1976, but some of the avionic sponsors did have new DME (distance measuring equipment) coming out. A few of the girls were able to talk the manufacturers into using the race to promote their products, even receiving enough funds to fly the race route as many as seven times before the race! Being East Coast girls we were lucky to be able to fly most of the route backwards, out to the start.

In order to ask for funding from strangers Paul created a business called "Bluegrass Flying Angels" an entity designed to promote women in aviation. Under that banner we hit breakfast clubs, radio stations, and any group willing to let us talk about the upcoming race. We were lucky to have our local bank fund a sizeable amount but we still needed quite a bit more. Then we hit on the idea that if we got enough people to donate $25 or more, we would provide them a picture of Laura and me in front of N80619 and present it to them at the end of the race. Somehow that didn't seem quite enough as some of our donors were just ordinary people, wanting to touch the exciting world of aviation in some way.

And then someone in the family came up with a

brilliant idea. Since we had the ability and materials, we could cut out four inch white vinyl stars and place them on the brilliant blue field of the engine cowl. Then at the end of the race we would take the star, with the sponsor's name on it, weathered and worn from racing, and put it with the framed picture of the two of us and present it to the sponsors.

Little did we know that forever more '619 would be adorned with the white stars, as we replaced them after each race, and she proudly wears them to this day. This always set her apart from all the rest of the similar Cessnas out there. Years later, as I visited some of those sponsors, I found the picture still proudly displayed on many living room walls, a living testament to their participation in my dream.

But now back to the beginning, back to '619 and her voice. Listening to planes overhead in the summer when I was little and living at the lake quite probably helped tune my ear to the differences in the sound of aircraft and I was anxious to hear what my new airplane sounded like.

On the first flight I flew in '619 she spoke to me in a contented purr, running smoothly in the run-up area, and then accelerating down the runway to lift off, and since it was a brand new engine with only ferry time on her, I conveyed to her that she was going to be a very special Cessna 172, and I could not afford the time to baby her engine. Therefore, she was going to be at two speeds only, idle and full throttle, so she had best get on with it. When I say she practically leapt into the air I am not exaggerating, but there also, for the first time, I heard her voice. Her voice was a very sexy rough growl that meant only business, and even a non-flyer would be aware she was speaking.

Any one who was alive during the beginning of television will remember the opening sound of one of the early dramas. The roaring sound of an airplane in a full dive, announced "Sky King"; the sound alone would create a rush to the tiny screen. The character, an Arizona rancher cum law enforcer, flew a series of Cessna T-50 Twin Engine Bamboo Bombers, each being replaced with newer aircraft as the series progressed. To this day when I hear a pilot hot-dogging it to the airport, the words, fully drawn out will escape my lips, "Skkyyyy Kiiinnngg". They say there are 'no old bold pilots', only those that have been extremely lucky, and those on a television series.

On that first flight with '619, I realized how thrilling it was going to be if we were accepted as racers. My home base at the time was Bowman Field, an old triangular former military base that frequently landed three planes at a time on its active runway. The first time we flew into the airport, the control tower recognizing we were strangers, gave us the middle or paved landing slot. The controller continually reminded us "do not turn off the active runway until we clear you. I repeat, do not turn off the active runway, land straight ahead and do not stop until the end of the runway. Wait there for further clearance." That was really scary the first time, since we had planes flying next to us and all of us came in about the same time for touch down.

But by the time '619 had arrived at Bowman, the airport was very familiar to me and I knew most of the tower operators. Seemed everyone on the field knew I had to get my commercial ticket to fly the Powder Puff, so it was not too surprising to have the tower operator congratulate me as I was returning from that first flight. Of course the guys in the tower knew I had passed my flight test and it was rather obvious I had bought the new Cessna, and besides word had spread quickly around the airport about the 'dollar down' bit.

As the tower operator was being so pleasant I pushed it a bit since I knew there wasn't much traffic at the moment, I said, "Tower, N80619 requesting a high speed low pass at Bowman". With a chuckle he gave me instructions and instead of reducing airspeed and lowering flaps to land, I pushed the throttle to the firewall and started my dive to the airport. That first time was such a kick as the wind blasted the aircraft and I felt the rush of blood and excitement while the plane appeared to be going on an angle to pile straight into the earth.

As I watched the altimeter unwind more rapidly than I had ever seen before, I picked the spot on runway 24 that I would pull up to fly level along the runway in front of the tower. As the earth rushed at me I had just a single thought that – oops! – maybe this just might not really work, never having stressed a plane like that before. But then with a hefty pull on the yoke we were level, and went screaming past the usual onlookers. Then it was time to pull up once again and reduce power for my instructions to exit the field to come back to land. I knew it had caused quite a stir at the Aero Club where there were always a bunch of onlookers watching and critiquing landings and it gave me a huge grin of pleasure.

Bowman Field, Runway 24, Louisville, Kentucky.
This is not the runway where we landed three abreast the
first time landing at this field, which is the runway perpen-
dicular to Runway 24. Tower is on the left at far end of the
line of buildings. Kentucky Flying Service is sort of midway
with the largest roof.

But what thrilled me most of all was her voice. I'd
had no clue it would rock me like it did, but hearing
the full out roar set my hair on end. It felt as if I had
truly been transported to another place in time, with
the sound opening my chest and filling my heart full,
and cracking my brain like it was on drugs. It was absolutely unbelievably awesome! My total body responded like I had never imagined to the roar of the
engine and wind, the force, the pure force of the dive,
pull to level, the race across the tarmac, and then pull
up to clear the airport, while reducing the speed. I
had been too engrossed to check how fast we had
been going! That was OK. It was only the first time,
and there would be lots more high speed, low passes
in the future to see how fast she could go.

I had now heard '619's voice and felt her power,

and the desire to race this beautiful creature was overwhelming. My instructor, Brooks, also fell in love with her and would fly with me in several races, her experience adding to my understanding of just how good this airplane was. But the first race was to be flown with my daughter, wise beyond her years in many ways, but still the next generation.

I wrote to Alice Hammond, the Civil Air Patrol Colonel who had so many years ago unwittingly told me that flying the Powder Puff Derby was the most exciting thing she had ever done in her life. Telling this icon that my daughter, who had also been a CAP cadet and was following in our aviation footsteps, was flying the race with her mother, all seemed very important to me. And somehow I think I wanted her approval and for her to share our excitement that we were going to be #112 to start, out of the two hundred planes accepted. Maybe I hoped she would send her wishes of 'good luck' to speed us on our way. But there was no answer back. Thinking the letter might somehow have been lost or she had been out of town I wrote her again of our good fortune after we were selected.

I watched the mail right up to the day we left on our miraculous journey and never got a response. We arrived in Sacramento for the start of the race, and several times I saw her across a room and headed to where she was but she was always gone by the time I made my way through the milling throng of racers, judges and officials. I was so disappointed, and thought the one time she saw me too, but it was forgotten as the pilot briefings, aircraft inspections and dinners took over my focus.

We even carved out time for a car load of us to find the way to San Francisco and see the sights and eat fresh seafood with sourdough bread on the waterfront and then ride the cable car. We were having so much fun and the excitement continued to build. But one of the days before the race we had to go out to the airport very early in the morning, to avoid the sun and heat to join many of the other racers in the final waxing of the plane and checking once again for anything that might be amiss since we had left her.

A few of the old time racers were willing to talk to the newbies, and in fact they were quite concerned that we stay safe. They did not give away their secrets but they spent time explaining what was likely to transpire, for instance, on our first time flying a timing line. Pauline Glasson was one of the old timers who spent quite a lot of time with the three of us, telling us that although all the girls involved were nice enough, almost any of them could be counted on to take every advantage they could, to beat us out.

It didn't matter whether it was flying a timing line or just getting in position in the morning line up for take-off. "Don't think that she won't crowd you so you miss the timing line and have to circle back around to cross it. Just figure if she can intimidate you she will!" It was playing chicken royally, just up in the air. We quickly learned it was much more cut-throat than even she had alluded to, but also so much fun.

Pauline was in her late sixties in that first race, but she flew everyday of her life doing aerial mapping and photography when she wasn't teaching students to fly. In all the races I flew with her she always started out with a newly certified student in the second

21

seat, and usually they were long-legged Texas beauties who could hold their own in any beauty pageant. Pauline was a tough Texas chicken without adornment except for her warm smile, and at the start of the race they were an incongruous pair.

What was fun, and what everyone tried to be there to see, was the end of the race when Pauline shut down the engine. Pauline would pop out full of energy, wearing a big smile, and unfazed by the three or four days of hard flying. Her poor younger partner would drag herself out the door looking like something the cat dragged in. The yellow rose of Texas would be drooping, with sweat-soaked hair, makeup and clothes. We never saw any of those co-pilots at a second race. We guessed once was enough.

Pauline lived to be 101 years old, flew 60,000 hours and was beloved by all who knew her. She was definitely one of the grand ladies of aviation, helping to enhance the role of women in aviation. She seemed quietly capable of leaping tall buildings in a single bound just like Superman, and she loved air racing, even though she was not what I think of as a hard core racer.

One thing I loved about racing Pauline was that our planes had the same handicap; this meant I was pitting myself against one of the best in head-to-head competition. We both had a Cessna 172M and I always kept track of where Pauline was, even though we might choose slightly different race routes, altitude and placement during the day of racing. I could always tell what I needed to do after seeing how our day stacked up against hers, and if I was a bit behind I knew I would have to make it up for sure the next day.

Whenever I would beat Pauline, I knew that the difference was not in pilot ability or pilot strategy, but in the planes themselves. I heard her plane cross the timing line one day when we had landed before she did, and I heard a much more muted voice without the bravado and roar than was present in '619. Feeling as I always did that '619 was not an inanimate object, but something with a soul, I knew she was the difference.

Although we never took a first, we always did extremely well. We knew the race really belonged to the larger planes or the twin-engine models with all the whistles and bells. In spite of all that, in our first race we placed well within the top third, coming in at the 65th position out of 200 which we felt was great for such neophytes.

That first race was a magnificent teaching tool. From losing an antenna, to landing in Lubbock just as the field closed down due to a huge thunderstorm, we learned how to fly. We learned those other racers really would not give an inch, just as Pauline had told us. We also learned that flying while wearing damp underwear and almost wet uniforms because they did not have enough time to dry thoroughly, was very uncomfortable.

We learned that roaring around at about five feet above the ground was indeed fun but also stressful. It was so hot the sweat blinded you while trying to see poles, wires, buildings and people. We had to fly low when we had a headwind, but it was only possible in mostly unpopulated areas. We learned that weather forecasts were to be taken with a grain of salt and that you really could learn to see and adjust the wind drift when it wasn't as forecast. So many things, so many lessons, but luckily we suffered no damage to aircraft or ourselves. But wow, did we learn!

Wilmington, Delaware, was ready for all the pilots at the end of that first race. We had endured great heat and uncomfortable situations. We flew between major thunderstorms, landing in cross winds the manual told us NOT to attempt! But – we had not run out of gas and we had found all our timing lines and were in one piece even after all of the scary parts.

One of the first people to greet me on arrival, much to my surprise, was Col. Hammond. With a grave look on her face she asked how the race was. When I said it was as exciting as she had said it would be and we had had an absolutely wonderful time, she finally smiled and said she had been so worried after I had written to tell her that I was flying with my daughter. She said that in her experience almost half of the teams ended up never speaking to each other again and she was so concerned that, especially as new racers, we might possibly encounter problems since she knew it to be so stressful.

Only then did I understand why she had avoided me and had not written back. Her words were reinforced by the outcome of just such a spat between two of the women with whom we had taken our written exams. They had been friends for twenty years, but had an argument and the pilot put the plane down in an empty field and made her co-pilot get out! So I understood how easily it could happen. I flew with three different co-pilots and thankfully we never had a disagreement that was worth mentioning. Mostly we just had fun and admired this beautiful country we live in as it unfolded beneath us.

Hydrating after landing at the end of the race, joyous we made it!

Brooks, too, had done well in that first race in her borrowed but new Cessna 182. Being faster than '619 we rarely saw her until the end of the day but then we could relax as we shared a room and dinner, after which everyone rinsed out their undies. Since weight was an extremely important 'go fast' factor we carried only what was on the 'required' list which included things like maps, logs and instrument navigation books called Jepps, and water. But personal stuff was pretty much only our toothbrush, camera, sunscreen and lip balm. Everything else was either needed for the plane or was deemed unnecessary. Oh, yes, there was always a little mascot tucked up by the windshield for luck, but other than those items, the flight was what most would consider bare bones. As to the mascot, once it was a tiny cloth alligator (as in 'see you later alligator', etc.) and since Charles Schultz's mother was involved in the race, almost all of us had Snoopy™ shoulder bags and so also sometimes had a small Snoopy Dog™ up in the corner of the windshield.

'619 started her life being prepped for that first race, but there was a lot of between race flying that taught me all about who she really was besides being a racer. I must admit it was hard to fly in normal cruise speed but we both did learn how to behave, even though it did not feel as comfortable, somehow. Like a few people I have met in this lifetime she had a heart of gold. In the time that she graced our home airport – in any of several different states – she took over six hundred people, young and old, for their very first plane ride.

They all fell in love with her as we explained just how she worked and what to expect when we taxied out for run-up, and gave her the necessary power for takeoff. With hand gestures, we showed what she would look like when we turned or banked, and about how we always watched for other planes in the air. But of course, first of all, we taught them how to buckle themselves in and where the bags were for airsickness. Only one person ever needed to use the bag, but he had been focusing a camera out the window for way too long a time, and had not listened to our warnings.

Paul taking a new flyer for her first ever flight.

These people new to flying never really heard her roar, just her gentle purr, and it seemed somehow she understood the need to be gentle with these new fliers, and even all her landings were whisper soft on touchdown. They would get out with a look like they would like to hug her but the human pilots would get the hugs instead, and I understood why they never left in a hurry but hung around for as long as they thought they could. Sharing her with these people, some that had been so afraid of flying, and especially in a small plane, was a great fun thing to do. I knew they would not be afraid of flying ever again and many would go on to become pilots themselves, which as far as I was concerned was a very good thing.

Chapter Two

For the uninitiated:

Transcontinental Air Racing is a 'motor' sport (as opposed to non-motorized gliders) that involves smaller general aviation airplanes competing over a fixed course, which may be a short course with pylons as markers, or over a long distance. Classes are determined by aircraft type and model, with handicapping based on the fastest time overall for each type and model, (the shortest actual flying time) or whoever finishes with the most points, or who comes closest to a previously estimated time. Pilot skill is not an official qualifier, but an experienced pilot will normally do better than a beginner. Some races make accommodations for two people in the plane (pilot and co-pilot/navigator) while others do not.

A racer's individual clock starts either when the flag drops or when the plane crosses a pre-set timing line and stops when the plane crosses the next one along the route.

In this kind of air racing if you are delayed it only adds time on the clock for that leg. If one misses the line the first time around, it is allowed to circle around and try again, but the clock is still running and there may be numerous planes attempting to fly the line. It is up to the pilot how much intimidation is used to make space flying the line, and one must remember they are flying at full power and speed.

The line itself is generally invisible, although pilots will have been given information as to its location before taking off at the start of the race. At each 'mandatory' airport (some are mandatory flybys and some mandatory stops) they establish this 'line' which is supposedly an easily understood and defined area that is given at pre-race briefings. It is understood that you must fly across that line (preferably perpendicular to the line as much as possible) in order to start or stop your own handicap clock.

It is sometimes really hard to find the line from the description given and more than once I could only hope that we had nailed it anyway. Generally, flying the timing line is the fastest MPH you fly during the race as you are usually diving from a higher altitude to fly mere feet above the ground across this arbitrary (invisible) line with full throttle. It is not at all unusual to have several planes trying to cross at the same moment and it can get really hairy since the width or length of the line often doesn't extend very far.

Then, too, the airport is still open to normal traffic at the same time, because the racers have to be allowed to land for fuel, so the placement of this line can be really weird. Then you have these planes diving at the airport with all that adrenalin spurting and the focus so total that one might not even notice another aircraft. Lots of fun, but not for the faint of heart!

Flying the Powder Puff Derby

Transcontinental Air Race program cover

Finally at the take-off for the start of the 1976 Powder Puff Derby, we lifted off into bright sunshine from Sacramento, a stream of multi-colored planes carving a slice into the blue that I imagine looked like a stream of bees heading from the hive. Some immediately powered to their highest altitude, while most of us spread out like an invading hoard. Two hundred planes, with only about thirty seconds separation, took off and after filling the sky, they seemed to dissipate like fog in the morning sun. I am sure the well-wishers on the ground felt bereft at losing the excitement that had been so great for so many days and was there no longer.

Sacramento Airport Tower

200 planes ready to race

Pre-race waxing while stacked in a long row of planes

Flat fields of the countryside before the mountains.

During that first leg to Fresno we lost sight of many of the other planes. The countryside was full of farms and orchards and our shadow was clear and defined on the ground. Flying our very first timing line at Fresno was quite a kick. We were finally in it – in the race – up to our necks. It was actually happening! The months of preparation and anticipation were over and we were actually racing.

I did not know '619 then, as well as I would eventually, but even so I thrilled to her diving at each timing line and then lifting to cruise to flying altitude looking for the next one. So addictive! It felt like we could do it all day, and that is exactly what we did. We changed our southward direction at Riverside and started heading northeast for our final leg of the day to the Grand Canyon. What had been a rather uneventful trip so far started to change.

As we approached the mountainous areas, we began to see heavy weather ahead. The thick cumulus clouds were dark and heavy in a line we would have to navigate. Making our way under the masses, the unexpected happened. As we crossed an area near

Kingman, Arizona, we were hit by lightning. **The world around us exploded!**

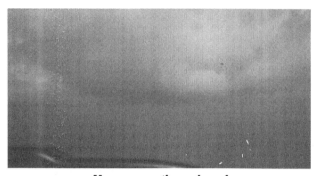

Heavy weather ahead

Without experiencing it yourself, it is impossible to know how wild it is for two pilots in a small aluminum craft to be targeted by a horrendously bright flash of lightning. All we wanted was to stay up in the air, and keep to an imaginary straight path leading to an invisible timing line on the ground! When our stomachs had righted and our shrieks had stopped, we realized a sort of undulating green glow had filled the front **of the** cockpit and spread out over the wings. It was magnificent, and so eerie that we both held our breath, waiting to see what might happen next.

Then we realized our instruments no longer worked properly. We had no compass, and the radios were inoperative. Consequently, we had no clue as to where we were or were to go. Staying on course as best we could seemed to be our only answer. But because of the storm we did not have much altitude and when you are flying not far above tree-top height, all that you can see is tree-tops. There were miles and miles of mostly evergreen pointed tips, with nothing

33

to say about where we were or which direction we were heading.

Finally Laura saw something on the ground that matched her map which told her where we were. Just about that same time, we came out of the worst of the weather and I could climb a bit higher to give her a better view. The largest clue, of course, was when we began seeing the terrain that indicated we were getting close to the Grand Canyon. Even though it stretches out for long distances, Laura was able to find the airport and we flew the timing line. Our radios came back on with a crackle and we circled back for landing. Here, the sun had been out all day and had heated the asphalt, while the dark pine trees had absorbed the heat.

The original rocks and rolls!

Approach terrain and Grand Canyon Airport

After landing safely at Grand Canyon, lots of smiles! Note Snoopy bag on my shoulder along with our overnight gear including all that was necessary to plan the next day's flight. Grand Canyon 'rocks' and Grand Canyon Airport were taken on our way out to the start of the race.

As I landed, with gratitude that we had made it safely, the plane lifted and then dropped, digging her tail tie-down ring into the black goo. The difference in heat absorption can be difficult to gauge at any time but we had just completed a tiring, excitement-filled day, and the St. Elmo's fire filling the cockpit had left me with few resources. Immediately after the tail tie-down ring was in the goo, it was released again which meant the plane launched itself for a small bounce or two before making the final joining with the pavement. I found tears streaming down my face, concerned that I might have damaged '619. She seemed to be her usual solid self as I taxied to the tie-down, directed by the race crew.

Suddenly the rest of all her instruments came back on line. At least we didn't have to worry about that overnight, and wonder if we would be able to race the next day. We were determined that we definitely would! Brooks was already waiting for us to find something to eat, so we shrugged off the day and began regaling each other with our individual exploits. Brooks said she was proud of her two students and that felt really good somehow.

The next morning the weather briefing seemed to offer only more marginal weather once we got started. The number of planes had thinned appreciably as the faster planes were much farther ahead, so it was hard to tell if they had been delayed anywhere by the iffy weather. There was a big map showing where all the planes were as of last night, but once dawn came up, we all scattered once again. I had seen the map the night before and realized we were still sort of in the thick of the racers. I knew that Brooks might have gone on to Lubbock the night before had she not waited for us. But still, I was glad she'd waited, as her bright smile had banished my tears about the hard landing.

Beautiful Santa Fe

We headed for Santa Fe, where we had stayed overnight on the way out. We hoped to just fly the timing line, get gas, fly the timing line again and head for Lubbock. It worked out well for us, although there were a huge bunch of planes there, **waiting and** hoping for better weather ahead.

Storm over Lubbock Airport, with plane flying timing line.

Lubbock. All the radio chatter said people were having trouble getting into Lubbock. When we arrived, I was surprised to be told to fly the timing line, as the storm line kept moving around the NDB (non-directional beacon) where we were to report our intentions to fly the line. When I say there was a big black wooly monster moving in and out you must believe that it was one scary dude.

We flew the line and as we circled back to land, the rain began pelting the aircraft and we could not even see the other end of the runway we were to land on. The rain had descended with a vengeance, thus shutting down visibility. We were the last plane to land. Those behind us we heard were being instructed to circle at various altitudes around the NDB and most were in hard IFR (instrument flight rules) and would stay there for more than an hour. Brooks had arrived before we did and ran out to hug our rain-soaked bodies. We had had to be sure the tie down chains were secure before we left '619 to the ravages of the storm.

Rain soaked ramp at Lubbock Airport

Eventually the storm moved a bit and the airport opened once again, first to let the poor stranded pilots in, some running low on fuel, and then to start funneling the rest of us back out to once again fly the timing line to restart our clocks. All the pilots' strategies were pretty much in disarray now. Ours had always been to get as far as we could, as soon as we could, in order to get to the end of the race in the four days allotted for the race. We knew we might not see Brooks again until the end of the race. It was imperative to finish the race and with this weather, there was a real possibility that we might not.

On the way to Oklahoma City we were flying low over the ground missing the headwind just above us, holding our course because Laura was so good at her navigating. Over the fairly flat and fertile land we encountered a fairly perplexing dilemma. A very large and long field was being sprayed either with fertilizer or bug repellent by a bright red crop duster making his way across the field from end to end. He would be directly in our path when we came even with him. Should we deviate left or right or over him when we got there? If you have ever watched a crop duster work, you'll note that when he gets to the end of a row and to be certain that he returns to his targeted area, he will pull up, bank either left or right and swoop down to start up again, next to where he'd left off.

I had no way to know for sure which direction he would go but we were going to pass him at the end of a row while he was making his turn. I was fairly certain I could count on him swinging left, having watched him as we approached, and I made my decision. We would go underneath the point where he pulled up, temporarily shutting the sprayer tanks off, to make his bank back to the field. It turned out to be a precision maneuver. He lifted up, we roared under and out the other side as he settled back down. In a fit of giggles, Laura and I realized that another racer was coming immediately behind us and that poor crop duster would be wondering just what was going on here. Where had we all come from and where were we going in such a hurry?

Oklahoma City was accomplished, gas tanks filled, and that was our overnight. The next morning after flying the timing line once again we were off to Little Rock. The Lubbock storm we had encountered earlier, we now encountered again. It kept us low underneath the roiling black stuff and we had a bit of trouble roaring across the tree tops once again and missed a checkpoint. As a result, we roared over the last little mountain only to realize we were on top of Little Rock! This time when I say we dove for the timing line I do mean we dove for it!

Jack had warned me about the propeller tips exceeding some critical speed in a dive like that, but I had no way of knowing at that moment if we did or not. He said that if there was a nick (a pretty constant hazard when you fly into small fields) the blade might come apart explosively or something similar. My thought as I pulled up from the dive was that I certainly hoped we had no nicks!

As we finally came shaky-legged to the gas pump I realized that with all the moisture and speed all the lovely white stars on our cowl had all started to peel back. This was a clear indication of the speed of that particular dive. It did not happen on any of our other races; that is, the stars trying to come off at any other time in the future. As the fuel was being pumped, we carefully put all the stars back flat once again, hoping they would hold for the rest of the race.

Next was Nashville, where the lovely southern belle at pre-race had said our timing line would be between the gold building and the orange towers. But when we found Nashville, we could not see the gold building or any orange towers at all. At 155 MPH you take what you can, and the only things we could see were two orange tires laying on the ground to the right of the runway. There was no gold building at all, so we decided to overfly the tires, hoping it would be close enough to something to stop our clock. We had no idea if it had been good enough but since we were given directions for landing we figured we must have done something right!

That gold building? Well, yes, it is gold when the sun shines on it, but it appears black otherwise. There was no sun shining on it that day! And those towers? They were indeed the tires, and 'orange' was the only thing that saved our bacon. As we headed for the gas pumps we saw Brooks and all her kids, in PPD tee shirts. They had driven down from Louisville to try and catch her and wish her luck. Because of that we were able to see her, too, as she had delayed her take off. Brooks was as much a southern belle as anyone I had ever met, and she, too, had a hard time knowing where the timing line was!

Brooks (second from left) with her crew that drove to Nashville. Great group of kids!

The race crew volunteers deserve enormous credit for making these races happen, but sometimes the balance is upset by a small but important incident that is really no one's fault. It gives one something to laugh about later, but for a while, there were quite a few steamed and upset pilots. Some arrived even sooner than we did, with their faster planes, and had even less time to make a decision.

Now there were only two legs left. Flying from Nashville to Parkersburg was sort of home territory for me. I knew the rivers and highways like an ant knows all of its own highways and byways. I had not yet flown into Parkersburg with '619 but I was quite familiar with the landscape. You start getting into the mountains a bit because after all it is *'West, by God, Virginia!'*

While I had frequently driven a car through similar areas on many occasions, I found it is quite different in a fast-moving plane that was running into more of the same nasty weather we had encountered earlier in the trip. It had pretty much kept pace with us, as it didn't have to stop for overnights. This is where we REALLY learned what the term 'scud running' meant.

Somewhere in the middle of the leg to Parkersburg we began to encounter the rain but an even bigger issue was the strong and chaotic winds. Parkersburg was our stop for the night, with a dormitory room at the college campus, but first we had to get into the airport! We flew the timing line with a hugely beneficial tail wind, but then, in order to land we had a heavily gusting wind coming off the left, almost perpendicular to the runway. The manual advises pilots to not even try to land in a cross-wind that high, but it really was the only place left for us to go within our fuel capacity. So we decided to try it, anyway.

In making a cross-wind landing you use a lot of rudder. Your feet really do a lot of the work. In this particular landing, Laura and I both knew I had to keep the left wing way low so the wind could not lift it and flip us over. She voiced her concerns that we would not make it but I felt strongly that '619 told me we could.

We tucked into the wind after the turn from base, and I reminded myself that I MUST keep that wing down and touch first with only the left wheel until the final roll out. Even then I could only taxi in a direction where the wind could not get behind or underneath us. Can you picture a plane landing tilted to one side with only one wheel touching all the way down the runway? Quite an operation and apparently there was lots of exertion and stress on my part.

With the rain slashing down on the windshield, we had trouble seeing anything by that time, but we made it to a tie down without flipping. We were picked up in a station wagon that would eventually take us to the college, but first, we had to check in with the race committee. The big map where the positions of all the planes would be posted was not up yet but there was a notice that one of the planes with two pilots had crashed and there was no word about their injuries as of yet. '619 had come through once again for us and we were safe on the ground.

The fog and rain did not go away during the night or by morning. At least the wind had abated somewhat. We waited and kept checking radar and weather because our pathway to Wilmington, Delaware, is through or over the Appalachian Mountain chain and it was not looking good. To stay VFR was going to be a huge challenge.

Finally, we decided we had to leave or we might never get through, and so we started. Anyone who has ever driven through the mountains has observed that on many of the highest parts there are towers. In fact sometimes they look like they have sprouted antennae of all sorts, looking like a bristly chin stuck out.

When flying, it is excruciatingly important to remember the existence of these protuberances, especially when you are tempted to just duck up and over that ridge and still stay below the heavy cumulus cloud. We call those ridges 'cumulous granite', where the moisture of the clouds above seems to blend in with the rock below and in between is the proverbial 'rock and a hard place'. The other thing one has to remember when flying ridges and canyons is that many of them lead to blind canyons. This ends up in

44

one *mell of a hess!!!*

How Laura got us through that day without crashing us into some of that beautiful granite is a feat at which I still marvel. We did not pull back the throttle, so at 155 mph or so we whammed through canyon after canyon unable to see the spine of the ridges as we passed, knowing they must be there in all that moisture. At the same time, we knew that if we ran into a blind canyon, we would have to discover whether there were towers on their ridge tops or not. Just maneuvering up out of a blind canyon might not **even be** possible.

Sometimes there was a river below and/or a road. Sometimes I had no clue *what* was below. I was too afraid of what was ahead! The flying was taking every bit of my energy and Laura was working hard to intuit the next turn. We had long since lost our bearings of where we actually were, and then suddenly we broke out of the last canyon and zoomed over a small ridge to blast **right over a small airport. We had exceeded minimums had we been spotted, but** we weren't there long enough, only a nanosecond, and Laura was pinpointing it on the map and calling for the turn to Wilmington.

The next instant it seemed we were flying the last timing line of the race, and once again, shaky-legged, we circled back to land. Looking up, finally, I saw that the grounds, and roofs, in spite of the drizzle, were all covered with spectators. I hoped Brooks had made it in and was part of the group, but I felt certain she had. I knew Paul was probably there waiting and worrying, too.

We had made it! Our first air race was behind us

and we had proved we could do it. It's the most satisfying feeling in the world!

At this point I would really like to acknowledge all the race crews, volunteers, CAP members, 99's and all the sponsors who helped make my dream a reality. All of my family was hugely supportive and understood what flying the Powder Puff Derby really meant. I was so lucky to have all the help I did to get where I wanted to go. Thanks to '619 for taking me along for the ride!

End of the ride, and oh, what a ride!

Chapter Three

That first race was 2,916 miles across this magnificent country of ours, and when we arrived home I started really looking into what might be going to happen next. Lunch with Brooks was a rehash of almost every one of those 2,916 miles, with many comments about what would be different in the next race. Neither of us questioned that there *would be* another race. Laura had gone back to school and her job, so she was left out of the planning for the coming year.

With the Powder Puff Derby at an end, there was a group starting a new race to take its place. It was to be called The Air Race Classic. Of course, there was an additional race, The Angel Derby that had been in existence for a very long time. We decided we needed to try both of those in the coming year.

While delivering the photos and stars to all the well-wishers who had supported us, I began to talk up the fact we were going to try two more races and would be looking for sponsors for those races. We now had a much better idea of what it would take as far as funds to fly a race, but at least this time, I already had the plane and the necessary qualifications to apply. Also, these races were of a smaller nature, so there would be fewer participants for the races we were considering. Being accepted would not be such a big deal as it had been for the first race. But it was all still very exciting!

# # #

And then Paul dropped the bomb. He was to start his new job in New Jersey the following Monday. Everything Brooks and I had started to work out for the races had to be set aside. We had been transferred once before, so I knew the drill and began at once to prepare and list the house with a realtor. We began telling friends and family of the move, and I began to cancel everything on my calendar with many apologies for letting people down. I knew Brooks would be upset, as we had become close friends and had started all those plans for the next year. I never envisioned, however, that she would be so angry that she would not even speak to me. It did not matter how many times I said it was not the end of our friendship, and that we would keep in close touch. Nothing I said made any difference. She just flat out refused to talk to me.

Paul came home after his first week in New Jersey and we had really looked forward to having the Thanksgiving holiday together. I wanted him to fill me in on what he had seen as far as housing, and what his new job and the people were like, too. He was tired and sat down in his favorite chair. I handed him a drink, and he took a deep breath in as he relaxed. Suddenly he gasped in pain. His back had 'gone out', probably from dragging his suitcase and briefcase in and out of the back end of the company car several times a day. He was in a very bad way.

No doctor was available due to the holiday, but our neighbor said his doctor, a chiropractor, was the greatest and he would get Paul in to see him. Do you know – or remember – how small a Chevrolet Monza Coupe was? Paul was a six-foot, solid-framed man, in great knee-bending pain. In spite of this, we had to get him folded up into that little sports car. He had a back brace band that was holding him together or we would have been unable to stuff him into the car at all.

There was no one in the office waiting room when we arrived first thing in the morning. Paul was ushered in to the examining room by the doctor himself. Paul then gamely sat perched on the edge of the examining table but the doctor told him he had to take off the band holding his midsection together, and in fact, just reached over and undid the Velcro attachments. At that point, Paul went into a spasm and crumpled to the floor, screaming with what was very apparent intense pain.

When he could breathe again, the doctor said we needed to get him on the examining table. We tried to get him standing up with many stops, waiting for the pain spasms to stop long enough to allow a bit more progress. It soon became obvious that even if we could get him upright, he could not tolerate the bending it would take to get him onto the table.

The doctor finally tipped the table up to its vertical limits and we almost managed to get him flat in between spasms when the doctor finally told us to stop. He then said he couldn't do anything for Paul unless he had something to relax him, but according to Kentucky law he could not administer such an injection. Paul would have to go into the hospital but the doctor said he would come and make the adjustments after Paul had had some pain relief.

I never knew if it was because of the holiday, or if

all hospital transport in Louisville was on a hardboard stretcher in a police station wagon. That was how our emergency call was handled. Two policemen walked in and strapped Paul to the board at some point while he was standing. In spite of his screams of pain, they tipped him horizontal to take him out the door.

I do not know who opened the door but the trouble started when it was discovered that the stretcher could not go through the doorway. The open slots that were designed as handholds for the police to carry the stretcher allowed a person to be on each side. There were no such slots at the ends, however.

Somehow the policemen each worked their way from the sides to opposite ends to make another attempt to get through the door frame. There was still not enough room, so they tried tipping the whole thing on its side. This nearly allowed Paul to slide off as there was a minimum of strapping holding him to the board. This action was accompanied by much more screaming.

Grabbing Paul's clothes to try and keep him on the board, they finally made it through the doorway and into a packed waiting room that had filled since we had first arrived. There were about a dozen wide-eyed patients awaiting the doctor, but one could tell they were all getting ready to bolt. Paul's screams of pain had been all too easily heard. In spite of his agony he kept saying as they tried to maneuver him through the outside door, "Honest, he never laid a hand on me!" As I followed the chaos of getting the stretcher into the back of the station wagon, I knew our neighbor would be in big trouble with his doctor friend.

Paul was admitted as a patient at the hospital and I knew he would be given the best possible care, but I truly had no idea what they could do for him, other than to give him shots for the pain.

The next day when I went to see him, they had decided to start Hydrocollator moist heat packs. Because of being short-staffed for the holiday weekend, he had been taken by wheel chair down to the therapy room, instead of having it done in his room. They must have given him LOTS of pain meds to accomplish that. However, I was there when he was brought back, so I witnessed the return.

The man in the bed alongside Paul's had a horrible infection on his leg. The huge bandaged foot and lower part of his leg were off the side of the bed, balanced on the top of a bedside chair as being elevated to drain was part of his therapy. He watched as Paul was wheeled up to the bed by Lurch, the attendant. I have no idea of what the attendant's real name was, as he was not one of the fastidious attendants and his name tag was nowhere in sight. His appearance though, and some of his mannerisms, likened him to the tall and lanky character in the sitcom, "The Addams Family," and so to all our family he was Lurch.

When it became obvious that Paul could not easily get out of the wheel chair and onto the bed, Lurch finally wheeled Paul around to the other side of the bed. He then raised the bed until it was just feasible for Paul to crawl cautiously from chair to bed. It was obvious Paul was in a great deal of pain but with glaring looks, he dared Lurch to rush him. When Paul was almost all transferred to the bed, Lurch hit the switch to let the bed down and turned to quickly leave the

51

room.

The cable began to unwind and yet the bed remained stationary as the corner of the roommate's chair back was keeping it from lowering. Since I was still out of the way by the door, I just pointed to what was occurring and Lurch turned back and with one swift move pulled the chair from under the edge of the bed.

Horror was mirrored on Paul's face, plus that of his room-mate, and my own, as the swollen and propped leg crashed down when the chair over-turned. At the same time, Paul's bed dropped almost a foot in elevation. When Paul could breathe again, the words uttered through clenched teeth let Lurch know in no uncertain terms that he would never let Lurch take him anywhere in a wheel chair ever again.

In the meantime, there was an effort to help his roommate get re-established to his elevated position with the aid of the nurses that rushed in when Paul screamed in pain. I spent the rest of the day trying to explain that Paul really was a very sweet guy, but I could tell the nurses felt he was 'one of *those* patients.' They had no idea what he was really like under normal circumstances.

The next morning I made my plane and hotel reservations for my Monday morning trip to New Jersey. As Paul was incapacitated, it seemed I would have to go and find a house without him so I took care of those details before I went to the hospital. Once there, I decided to stop by the cafeteria on the lower level to get some coffee to take upstairs but as I was heading to the elevator there were two nurses in laughing hysterics standing nearby.

As I waited for the elevator I heard the words, "Honest to God, he was going too fast and hit the center framework of the door and LAUNCHED him right off the gurney into the air!" Oh, no! But I would learn all about that episode, too. Paul had related to me how Lurch's long legs made him the Marathon man and Paul could feel his hair blown back as they had flown down the corridors with Paul hanging on for dear life to the wheelchair handles.

Whatever good relaxation that had been accomplished in therapy was blown away on the trip back to the room, thus Paul had said no more wheelchair rides with Lurch.

Not knowing what I would find when I got to the room, I nevertheless mentally prepared myself as best I could for whatever I would find. As I walked into the room his roommate saw me and cried, "You will never believe what happened!"

"He was launched off the gurney," I said. "It is all over the hospital as the funniest thing that has ever happened." But I was looking to see if Paul was indeed even still alive and breathing. He was, although quite pale and his face pinched with obvious pain.

According to his roommate they had filled him with enough drugs to relieve an elephant of pain. I had the errant thought that maybe between the bed drop of the day before and then this new insult to his body, was it possible that whatever was out of place in his back was now back in place? No, probably not, but it was a good thought.

I arrived at the Newark Airport before dawn on Monday and finally found the company car that had been left for me. Without much of a map, I made my way to the Mt. Arlington area where Paul had found homes that we could possibly afford. They were a long way from his job though, and the taxes on such a home would blow me away, but my first task was to find a reasonably-priced house.

The company required that I work with a real estate agent, and so we met and traipsed from location to location. Figures swirled through my mind with confusing and amazing speed. The type of house we had been able to afford in previous moves, was now were so far out of our reach in this NJ economy that I knew it was not going to be good.

Finally, I gave up for the day, and found the motel which wasn't too far from the last house I'd looked at. Even though it was a large motel chain, I still felt a bit uncomfortable and very vulnerable. In those situations I always tell myself to buck up, it will all work out and I was probably perfectly safe.

I left my room earlier than planned the next morning and it was a good thing. As I stepped out into the parking lot I finally saw the company car. Unfortunately, it was much lower than when I left it. Due to the fact, of course, that it no longer had any wheels. Great welcome, New Jersey, I just feel all the love!

I was a long distance from the Zone office so it was a good part of the day before I had wheels again. Finally, however, some-one did come and rescue me. The situation did not get a whole lot better after that, except that out of desperation, I finally chose a house just so I could get back to Kentucky. I knew Paul was still in the hospital, and in fact he spent ten days there, but I was hoping the other parts of my life were doing better than he was. I am so glad I did not know then, that New Jersey for me would not ever get much better.

Whenever we were transferred, it was my job to take care of all the details. Paul, already at his new job was always focused on working and learning the ropes, so I learned about moving companies, policies and schedules, all the while starting the sorting and packing in one place while getting power, phone and other utilities lined up in the next place. Usually there was a yard sale of some sort, but for this move there was simply not time.

In fact, even my plan of flying '619 to her new airport before the move was quashed because the company wanted us to be moved before the end of the year. That was less than a month to sell and buy and move. Our daughter Laura was still in school at Western Michigan, but would soon have Christmas break. Our son Tom had changed his plans the year we moved down from Michigan; he planned at first to take his senior year at his previous school but changed his mind and finished up in Kentucky. He had graduated after needing just a semester, and decided he could at least help us get moved into New Jersey before he figured out where he wanted to go. Without the two of them, I doubt we would have made it.

When the moving van pulled out of the house in Kentucky, Tom accompanied Paul to the airport for the commercial flight to New Jersey. Paul was still not fully functional, and it killed him not to be able to do anything to help, not to mention needing Tom's assistance most of the time.

I met Laura on Route 80 midway for both of us and she followed me to the exit for Lake Hapatcong. A

New Jersey state trooper came up behind me just as I signaled my exit and followed me with lights on until I could get entirely off the road for safety. I had no clue what he was stopping me for and all he said when he came up was the usual 'license and registration' command. I already had them out and started to hand them to him when he reached in to take them from me. Bad move.

Since you cannot put flammables and paint and the like in a moving van, I was pulling a small trailer, covered with a tarp, one that we had had for the previous three moves. Inside the little Monza all sorts of things were jammed in with just enough visibility to be legal, and residing on the front passenger seat sat our mean-tempered, little three-pound poodle, who by the way, did not like the hand reaching in the window. She was also short sighted, or maybe even a bit blind, but oh! Was she fast!

She latched onto the trooper's hand which had taken the identification, and the pieces flew up in the air and landed nowhere that I could see. He cursed just as Laura arrived to find out why I had been stopped, and that complicated the issue further as he, I imagine, thought my reinforcements had arrived. It took a while to find the identification bits, allow the trooper to get calmed down and then to ask all the weird questions. Weird because we had no idea yet as to why he had stopped me.

For a time, it seemed we would have to unload the packed car and trailer unless I could prove I was just moving into New Jersey. To me it was obvious we were moving, but until I found some paperwork for the power company deposit, the trooper was not explaining. And still, we didn't understand what he was, in fact, looking for. Finally, he said it was because my trailer did not have a license plate! However, it was obvious there had been one at some time, because you could see the outline and lack of paint.

I told him Kentucky did not require plates on garden trailers and I had to take it off, but when we had been in Michigan we had had to have one. So simple. All that fuss could have been saved if he hadn't been so New Jersey trooper-ish. Ah, yes. My second 'Welcome to New Jersey' and I could tell it was not going to be so easy finding my way. New Jersey did not like me and it was reciprocated big time.

Laura and I met Paul and Tom and we waited in the creaky empty house for our furnishings to arrive. Not having the phone installed yet complicated things when the blizzard hit. The movers could not let us know that one of the dual tires on the truck had caught fire. They had to stop, and move the smelly burned rubber duals into the van before they could continue. When the snow started and they weren't there yet, we realized that we had better get something to keep them from slipping and falling. We bought a good many fifty pound bags of sand and stacked them up by the front door.

The crippled van arrived in snow so blinding we almost missed seeing its arrival. The drivers were exhausted but since it was Christmas Eve they were determined to get the van unloaded and get back to their families in Kentucky. Tom and Laura became their helpers and slipped and slid with the drivers in the dark blowing snow to get everything into the house, tracking the snow and sand inside with every step. We used all the sand, finding that it had to be continually re-scattered to have any traction at all, and over the four years we lived there the vacuuming was always accompanied by the continual sound of gritty sand being sucked up.

The drivers were on their way finally and would get home before Christmas was over so we all were pleased. We were left with the aroma of burned rubber in the air, gritting sand under foot and complete exhaustion in our souls. It was hard on Paul to have to sit and do nothing, but since he still had to use pain meds on a daily basis he really did not argue over much. I had not flown '619 or heard her voice in ever so long, and did not know when – if – I ever would again. Welcome to New Jersey.

# # #

Once things began to settle down, I looked for work that would support keeping '619 and also the racing habit I had decidedly acquired. Of course I had to first find a home for '619 but more importantly I had to make arrangements for her to fly to New Jersey. There were lots of places I could tie her down not far from the house, but airports are also home to wayward pilots seeking their like kind. So a home for '619 would also be a second home for Paul and for me. It would be a place to make friends and learn about our new territory and where we would feel, in time, our most comfortable.

The closest airport surprisingly seemed to be the best fit according to my research. I then began to search for the aircraft mechanic who would do annual inspections and also the rigorous paperwork for the two races. He could not be too far distant and had to be really sharp yet not too expensive. That meant he would probably not be connected to an airport as such, but an independent mechanic with great credentials. Now, that was quite a tall order as I knew nothing much about the area or who was who in the zoo.

I discovered, though, that the best engine mechanic around was a free-lancer who just happened to be at the chosen airport, and that fact quite blew me away. I started to forgive New Jersey a wee bit for my not-so-pleasant introduction to the so far unfriendly state, and set out to meet my new mechanic.

I had heard his office was in a grounded semi-trailer on the south side of the airport, so I parked at the airport office and decided to first secure a tie down at the office for the day when '619 would arrive in New Jersey, whenever that would be. Two birds, as the saying goes.

The door to the airport office opened onto a large room that was filled with square tables each with four chairs adjacent to a long bar with high stools filling one area off to the side. A well-used piano had a spot at the end of the bar and it was apparent to me that there was food, and from the luscious smell, great food available at this little rural airport.

A smiling pony-tailed woman in a floury apron came from the back and asked what she could fix for me. Wow! It looked like this airport would be a great fit. Looking out at the large field with a wide variety of planes tied down in the short grass, I could see finding a spot was not going to be a problem either.

Once I had paid a month's rent and secured a spot to tie '619 down, and had answers to all my questions about local etiquette and the price of fuel, I left and headed to where I thought I would find the mechanic. On the way I ran into a man whom I guessed was a mechanic from his demeanor alone, but I stopped him and asked if he was Jack. With a look that said 'who wants to know?' he said he was. I introduced myself as a new tenant at the field, that my plane was coming from Kentucky, and I needed his services when it arrived to get it ready for the upcoming race. Would he be willing to help me? "No," and that was his one word, but very definite, answer.

And he turned abruptly and continued on his way. Oh, great. I had thought things were working out really well finally and then I literally ran into a stone wall. I could tell Jack was an independent cuss and had no problem telling future customers to go fly a kite. Only this lady wanted to fly a race not a kite.

For a week I was on the phone with various service operations and all recommendations kept pointing back to the man who would not give me the time of day. So I made another trip out to the airport and found him working on the brakes of a neat looking plane inside the hangar. Since I was standing over him while he worked, I decided it was a good time to confront the man. I would not, could not, take his 'no' for an answer. When I told him I wanted to talk to him, and would stand there until he did, he finally, after finishing what he was working on, rolled out from under and stood.

I asked him again if he would be my mechanic for '619 and he again said, "No."

"But why not?" was answered with "I don't work for crazy ladies that fly, especially that fly air races."

Whew! And where did that come from. At least now I had an idea of what the problem was, and now I could work on a solution. Eventually we had an actual conversation and by the end of it he had agreed to consider working with me, but I could tell with any misstep, he would bolt. The racer he had once worked with was apparently a real piece of work and really left him with a permanent bad taste and dislike of women racers, and I assumed, female pilots too.

But still, I had to get '619 to New Jersey. I had been hired into Avionics Products and could not take the time off from the new job to go pick her up. The ideal solution would be for Brooks to fly '619 in and then take a commercial flight back to Louisville, but she still wouldn't talk to me. Finally, I called Dick, her boss, and explained what I needed. And – at last, she was convinced to open up again to me. She finally agreed she had an open schedule toward the end of January, and would come. I could barely wait for her to get there. And I was anticipating hearing the be-loved growl of '619 once again and seeing my flying friend. It would be so good!

Soon life would be livable again. I was enjoying my new job with good people, and soon all would be right in the world. I would be able to get up in the air with my beloved plane and my new life in New Jersey would really begin.

# # #

Finally, the day arrived when I could go to the airport and wait for Brooks and '619 to arrive. The weather was very iffy as the temperature was hovering near freezing and it varied from a light mist to a drizzle. The almost-freezing temperature meant there was a real concern for icing to build on the airframe, and the wings in particular, and although I knew Brooks would file an IFR flight plan, she might run into a patch of freezing rain that could change her situation drastically. Of course it also meant she might not be able to land at my airport but would have to go to another airport that had an IFR approach and better weather.

Morristown was the alternate and about a thirty minute drive from Flanders Valley Airport, but I really wanted '619 to come into her new home. I knew some of the locals at the airport were sort of waiting to see this plane that had flown in an air race to come in with this female Kentucky pilot.

I had talked about Brooks and who she was, but Saturday was a pancake breakfast event that people came to regularly and caught up on all the latest gossip, so there was already a bit of curiosity about the newest tenant. Quite a few knew Jack had snubbed me at first contact and wanted to see what had changed this oft times stubborn-minded and independent character. I must say I never learned why his stance on helping me had changed.

In the dripping and murky air there suddenly came the sound I had been waiting to hear. The approach for the most often used runway direction was difficult, because one had to fly the fairly steep ridge of the mini-mountain that blocked the eastern approach and then pull power and lower full flaps to drop on the very end of the runway. Since the length of the runway was only 1700' and the last half took a real downward turn, it was necessary to plant the wheels as close to the approach end as possible, the end by the ridge, or the propeller would harvest the corn in the field beyond.

That happened quite frequently because there were also very scary high-tension wires capping the ridge, and they had a tendency to fill a pilot with the well-known 'pucker factor'. So in addition to the murky, nasty weather and it being an unknown field, Brooks had to make a difficult landing without knowing for sure what the runway conditions really were. There was no tower at Flanders Valley Airport. Fortunately she managed the near icing on the runway with skill and taxied back to the turnoff quite gracefully. '619 was home and all was right with the world.

The hug that Brooks and I then experienced definitely erased all her anger at me. There is nothing like having a really rough flight to make one glad to be alive and to forgive any ill feelings of any kind. Something about putting your feet on solid ground re-establishes how precious life and friends really are. Forget the small stuff – and it *is* all small stuff, isn't it?

Chapter Four

1977 Angel Derby   Racer #28

1977

ALL WOMEN'S INTERNATIONAL AIR RACE "ANGEL DERBY"

OHIO STATE UNIVERSITY AIRPORT, U. S. A.   to

FREEPORT INTERNATIONAL AIRPORT,   THE BAHAMAS

SPONSORED BY

BAHAMAS MINISTRY OF TOURISM

ALL-OHIO CHAPTER OF THE NINETY-NINES

ALL WOMEN'S INTERNATIONAL AIR RACE, INC.

SCHEDULE

Impound Deadline, Ohio State University Airport . . . . 1700 EDT, May 4, 1977
TAKEOFF, Ohio State University Airport. . . . . 0930 EDT, May 8, 1977
RON, Fort Lauderdale Executive Airport. . . . . 1900 EDT, May 9, 1977
FINISH DEADLINE, Freeport, The Bahamas. . . . . 1200 EDT, May 10, 1977
AWARDS BANQUET, BAHAMA PRINCESS, Camelot Room . . . . . 2000 EDT, May 13, 1977

DESIGNATED ENROUTE AIRPORTS   St. Mi's

  1. Ohio State University Airport, Columbus, Ohio (RACE START)
**2. Dress Regional Airport, Evansville, Indiana 278.06
**3. Barkley Field, Paducah, Kentucky. 95.70
 *4. Greenville International Airport, Mississippi 276.74
**5. Dannelly Field, Montgomery, Alabama 279.11
**6. Gainesville Municipal Airport, Florida. 303.44
 *7. Fort Lauderdale Executive Airport, Florida (RON) 272.78
  8. Freeport International Airport, The Bahamas (RACE FINISH) 94.41

                                                                    1600.24

**Must Flyby, Designated refueling airport
*Must Stop, Designated refueling airport

Eventually, as usually happens, the storm passed and sunshine came once again. It helped with the winter-induced depression, plus being able to fly my baby once again added to the feeling that life was good. Brooks and I finished planning the two races we were going to enter, and by the time I put her on a plane for home, my life seemed to be so much better. Maybe I would survive after all.

Pre-race inspection being started by the inspectors

As I gathered the necessary paperwork together for the two races, I spent as much time at the airport as I could. In addition to getting acquainted with all the unique characters, there was also the time spent working with Jack on the aircraft mechanicals and paperwork for which he was responsible. I had found a job related to aviation and discovered the local personnel were also interested in the coming air races, which made the time I spent working on the preparations less of a problem.

Again I was already working to find sponsor money and although the company itself could not be a sponsor many of the employees did donate. When I came home from the first race, Paul unveiled my new license plate they had bought to commemorate the race. They'd decided on a unique one that said, "K FLIES", and the fact it adorned my Corvette might have made it seem that I was thumbing my nose a bit at the cops, when in fact they were just honoring the other part of my life.

That was an interesting thing about driving in New

Jersey. In spite of – perhaps because of – the air racing, I had always been a pretty prudent driver. But once I was integrated into the normal traffic of New Jersey, I found I was always speeding, mostly just to keep from being run over!

Our access route to work was Route I-80, three lanes of impatient, discourteous drivers, and I learned to ride in either outside lane but never in the middle, and missed accidents many times because of this strategy. I did not particularly like the feeling of Russian roulette when I was driving and did not even like the fact I was speeding all the time. Life was too precious to take so many chances. Especially when on the ground.

The crew at my new airport starting getting into the excitement of preparing the plane and sponsorships ready to go, and they decided to have a *bon voyage* hangar party that would allow people to contribute to the pot, while also having a good time, too. It turned out to be a humdinger of a party with the airport owner banging out tunes on the office piano that had been moved out to the hangar, where people sang off key with gusto. The food created by the little airport restaurant had a surcharge that went into the pot, but the special thing at the main table was a huge sheet cake that someone had very accurately airbrushed '619 from our photos, complete with bright colors and good wishes on the race. It was almost too pretty to cut!

'619's cake!

Jack and his wife, Dot, cutting up, with me in the middle!

There was a throng of people at my leave-taking and as '619 lifted off the end of the runway I could hear the cheers over her rumbling voice. I was headed into rather iffy weather on my way to Kentucky to pick up Brooks. Weather forced me to land at the small county airport of Beaver Falls, PA, until the visibility increased, but that did not dampen my enthusiasm, and when I arrived at my old stomping grounds, Brooks was there to belatedly greet me. It really felt great to be walking into Kentucky Flying Service once again, and be greeted by old friends.

Brooks and Kay, new sponsors on the stars and plane.

Gathering of KFS friends in the hangar before leaving for the race with Brooks.

The race brought out how much Brooks and I enjoyed each other's company and also helped to reassure Brooks that distance would not damage our friendship in any way. Because I seem to be able to navigate and interpret winds and ground track exceptionally well, we ended up with Brooks doing the flying, while I would do the navigating.

That first race together, she too, became aware of how unusual '619 seemed to be, and how much more capable she was than the service manual said she might be. '619 had a service ceiling of 12,000 feet, and although Brooks, because she was a smoker had to put on her oxygen mask at 10,000 feet, the plane easily kept on climbing past 14,500 feet, so the grasping fingertips of the mountain would not rip her belly open. Of course, had it appeared we might be going to crash, Brooks would have banked away from our trajectory. Yet time and time again, the aircraft performed flawlessly, carrying us safely away from harm yet allowing us to keep to our selected route. '619 continued to amaze me every day sometimes in not so subtle ways.

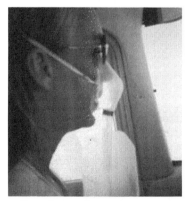

Brooks on her oxygen – scaling some of the higher peaks.

Ken Wallace, a P-51 Mustang pilot/owner from California, wrote lovingly on the soul of an airplane, about the feeling he and others have regarding the unlimited nature of certain airplanes they had flown. It reiterates all I have said and felt with regard to these cylindrical metal tubes of inanimate matter that seem to be able to do more than one could dream.

At the same time, there is also a connection to my heart and soul that is almost inexplicable. I find that I keep trying to write about it because it is so fascinating to me. Maybe her voice set up a vibrational frequency the first time I heard it that connected into the center of my being and allowed belief of limitation to be superseded by the wonder of possibility. I do know that fear did not fly with me, except rarely, and those few occasions were when I might have exceeded good sense in some way, but I always expected she would make it right in spite of me. She always did.

News Release Excerpt:

1977 Angel Derby "The Race with a Goombay Beat" May 8-10, 1977 Columbus, Ohio to Freeport, Bahamas

From Ohio State University across eight states, Angels will speed across a finish line sometime before noon on May 10 at Freeport International Airport.

Sporting such un-angelic equipment as propellers, struts and landing gears, these fearless she-eagles will be competing in the 27th Angel Derby, an international all-woman air race which knows no boundaries and is open to women pilots from anywhere in the world. Taking to the skies to prove that airplanes can perform beyond their maker's fondest dreams these high-octane ladies must observe a myriad of flight regulations and call upon all the skills they have developed from their first hour of flight instruction through their highest ratings. Precision is a must, a couple of miles off course is too much.

Any woman holding a Private Pilot Certificate with Instrument rating and flying a stock, unsupercharged, fixed wing aircraft of between 145 and 570 horsepower is eligible to compete. The Derby is judged on a handicap basis and is won on the judges decisions in relation to times and regulations.

Again, even in this press release the idea that planes can surpass "the maker's fondest dreams" is a theme I whole-heartedly accept. This was the shortest race that we flew as far as length, because it was only 1600 miles. Most of the races were longer, at least another thousand miles or so. But that did not keep it from being one of the most difficult races, and it was weather that was the demon.

I flew from New Jersey to pick up Brooks but fog grounded me half-way there. I waited for it to clear and finally reached Bowman Field, Kentucky, but Brooks and I had to overnight there instead of heading for the race start as the whole Ohio Valley was full of dense moisture in one form or another. Extremely low visibility was pervasive and airports would be open one minute and have to close five minutes later. We finally reached Columbus and were in time for the start of the race but it was an insistent warning of what was to come.

Racer #28 starting the Angel Derby

All the races I participated in flew by VFR rules. This means one needed to have three miles visibility and be clear of clouds, and that meant carefully-laid plans often went sideways. Everyone knew that if you were caught at less than the minimums, you would be disqualified. In addition, the FAA frowned on it, too. But in this particular race there were many pilots who did just that, in spite of possible consequences. The weather for the whole race stayed iffy, and by that I mean we saw very little calm, clear, sunny weather.

"ANGEL DERBY"

May 8, 9, 10, 1977

Looking
Good!

NEWARK
ZONE

BLUEGRASS FLYING ANGELS, INC.

For this Race, called the Angel Derby, we had put new race numbers on the plane, changing from the #112 to #28, and all the stars were replaced with new sponsor's names on them. The Powder Puff Derby stars had already been framed with the photo of Laura and me beside the plane and given with thanks to the various sponsors of the PPD. Our gratitude was great to these individuals and companies for helping us achieve our dream. This is the photo for the 1977 Angel Derby which was put into a frame, with the tattered star for this next group of sponsors.

Our first "fly by" (at the timing line that stopped the clock and restarted it as well, if you were not stopping for fuel) was in Evansville, IN. The field had to close every so often because of the fog, so the racers were already getting spaced out. By the time we reached Paducah, KY, the tension caused by that bad weather was almost as thick as the moisture all around us.

Luckily Paducah was home territory to us, and we knew it well, so it did not bother us as much as some of the other racers. Our problem was on the next leg to Greenville, MS, and the storm that now raged around us tossed our tiny plane wickedly about like a potato chip.

We were flying only about 500 feet or less above the ground to stay VFR but even so I still could not make out all the landmarks. Soon our location was so generalized that we'd broken out across the Memphis Naval Air Station before I could pinpoint our location with any accuracy. We knew where we were by then, but felt lucky there had been no incidents. Because of the weather, I doubt if there was much training going on, anyway.

The biggest problem we encountered up to that point was extremely rough winds. Then came one gust that twisted the aircraft so severely that the baggage door popped open. Suddenly, one of the five-pound Jeppesen IFR Manuals from the back baggage area slammed into the back of my head!

Well, we could not continue with the door open so I crawled over my seatback and the other seats and tried pulling the door closed. No dice. The frame was twisted enough that it would no longer close tightly. I remembered seeing a cord on one of the duffle bags. After I'd unknotted it and wrapped it around the door latch, I then pulled it as tightly closed as I could get it, and tied it to the back seat. All the while I was doing this, I was being slammed into all parts of the plane by the turbulence.

Naturally, by the time I was able to get back into the front seat, our location was merely a wild guess. I did spot a railroad track and told Brooks to hang tight on that until I found something else I could pin-point for a location. We actually found Greenville down the railroad tracks with no trouble and flew the timing line, grateful to land and get gas and straighten out the mess inside the plane.

One thing I haven't mentioned is that our normal navigational instruments could sometimes be rendered absolutely useless – if you were below or out of range, or if a storm has knocked them off line for a bit. This is why knowing where you are in relation to landmarks on the ground can be valuable. No, it's more than valuable, it's a friggin' necessity especially in wild weather like this!

Once on the ground I quickly discovered that no matter how hard I tried, the baggage door simply would not close tightly. Soon, hot wet tears for my injured baby began rolling down my cheeks. She did not deserve to be damaged, but for the moment we could do nothing but call it a night because there was not time to get back in the air and get to Montgomery, AL, before sunset.

The next morning the weather was still bristly, but we filed our flight plan and took off. In the middle of the leg we ran into more of the same turbulent storm clouds, dark and heavy with rain. They were the same sort that had twisted the tail so badly the day before, but much to our surprise when we landed, the rope was looser and I realized the door would now close tightly! More tears but of gratitude this time.

After the Montgomery fly-by to start the clock, we headed off for Gainesville, FL, knowing we had to reach Ft. Lauderdale before sunset. Although it didn't seem there was much clearing of the nasty stuff, our hopes were high. It wasn't long before we realized that we had caught up to the slow-moving, pervasively bad weather.

Flying the timing line in Gainesville we could see the airport might shut down at any time but we needed to top off our gas before continuing on. Once on the ground we saw there were quite a few planes from the race all bunched up, down by the operations building. That did not bode well, as most of them were faster planes that should have been gone by the time we arrived.

We added '619 to the accumulation of race planes and headed inside to see what the situation might be, and found really disgruntled pilots discussing the pros and cons of the weather. We checked for ourselves and realized there was no way our slower plane could beat the weather that was now most decidedly moving across our path.

Some of the pilots decided they were going to risk it and headed out to take off, but the majority of us continued milling about. It soon became obvious that all those who were standing there with us would be disqualified from the race for not having made it to Ft. Lauderdale by sunset. The weather had beaten us.

There would be no Freeport, Bahamas, for us tomorrow or banquet or prizes or anything.

Having raced with many of the group in the Powder Puff Derby the year before, we knew the other girls were all pretty good sports so we set about trying to create something good from it all. Almost half the 96 women entered in the race were sitting there with us, fighting disappointment at not finishing.

By the end of the night, the group had transformed our "I Flew the Angel Derby" tee shirts with dark blue marker pen. We took the "F" and turned it into a "B" so it now read "I Blew the Angel Derby." Then someone else came up with the idea of forming an elite club called the "Stalled Angels" to denote our singular status and how selective it was.

Brooks, her daughter Jane, and me on the left.

77

Racers making the best of it by forming an elite if disgruntled group. We had opted for safety and had stayed on the ground and were all disqualified.

Brooks was the one who decided on and implemented a monogrammed patch, and when we arrived home she had them made up and sent to all the girls with our distinctive status. We wore them proudly on our jackets to every race after that.

We decided to go along with a group to find a hotel to stay the night. Since Brooks and I were not due back home for a few more days, she suggested we indulge in some R&R at the home of her Aunt Jane and Uncle Max in Jacksonville. Maybe we could even get some sun at the beach.

Of course, the next morning the weather was beautiful. We were both beach lovers and Max and Jane truly seemed pleased to have us barge in on them. It *almost* made it worth missing the end of the race. And besides, it gave us more time to talk about the next race.

Chapter Five

Air Race Classic 1977   Racer # 22

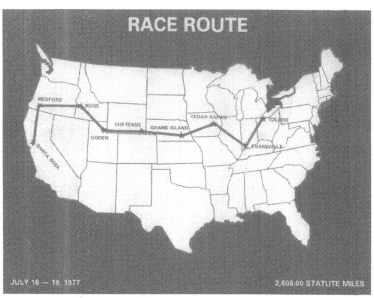

Two months later, I was once again on my way back to Louisville to pick up Brooks. We took off to fly the first ever Air Race Classic route in reverse of what the race would be. We made our way out to Santa Rosa, CA., where the actual start of the race began. Following the route backwards gave us a preview of what we would encounter on the actual race. On the early part of our journey we had some tough weather but the western half of the country was beautiful.

Brooks peering out at the snow covered peaks.

The only clouds we encountered on the journey from Boise to Medford were in a wreath circling Mt. Shasta, the stately peak glistening with snow even

though it was mid-July! It was an awesome sight making us, in our little metal tube, feel very insignificant and vulnerable. I noted that the peak was 14,162 feet high, but the whole of the Cascade mountain range was making '619 work hard to overfly the thin altitudes high above the treacherous rocks beckoning below. They seemed to be reaching up to snare our feet and pull us down.

'619 was as magnificent as were the mountains and never skipped a beat taking us to safety beyond, her engine growling in defiance of their supremacy as she climbed up and over their reach. I loved her more each minute.

# # #

Brooks's father, William F. Lucas, was a former CEO of Brown-Forman distillery, a producer of quality alcoholic products that was founded in 1870 by George Garvin Brown in Louisville, KY. Before we left to head west for the start of the race, Brooks received an invitation for us to visit the Korbel Winery in Guerneville, CA, for the day between the mandatory pilot briefing and the actual start of the race. The invitation included a luncheon prepared by one of the owner's family members and would take place in a lovely residence located on the hills above their beautiful sales building, replete with swimming pool and a view of grape vines gracing every bit of the rolling hills.

Brooks relaxing and sampling the wine.

After a tour of the winery, we found ourselves relaxing in the charmingly-appointed home, where we had our own personal wine-tasting session during an absolutely delightful gourmet lunch.

The food, the wine and the company was great!

After spending the afternoon sprawled lazily, half soused, by the pool, it was extremely hard to tear ourselves away at the end of the day and go back to face the grueling days of racing. *I know, poor baby, such a life to which you were subjected.* What a blast! The winery was awesome! If ever you are in the area, you shouldn't miss it!

The weather for the race was given with many warnings that the various models were not in agreement, not so much regarding rain and possible IFR conditions, but the winds appeared to have been stirred with a stick on the maps. This has a great bearing on route planning, but we thought we were in good shape for what was to come and felt we could fly the timing line at Boise without stopping for gas as we had had a terrific tail-wind forecast.

Often, you lose time climbing out after a fuel stop, because you have not allowed enough time to be at full power to re-cross the timing line. It always seems that the hurry is greater when trying to get started on the race route. Whereas, if you are only flying the timing line, and don't plan on landing, you are already at max speed when you cross the line to stop the time of that last leg. Also, the leg from Boise to Ogden was a bit shorter than Medford to Boise. So, we thought, what had we to lose? Nothing, except to run out of gas and crash.

During the race briefings there had been a warning from the race committee about being very careful of the toxic salt water adjacent to the Great Salt Lake that we would cross on our way into Ogden airport. No matter what, or whatever the circumstances, *do not land* in the pretty colored water as it most likely would mean death. Of course, no one expected they would even have to consider that as we all were so very intent on our race preparations, and knew what we were doing. Of course we did.

Condensing, but toxic, salt ponds.

We quickly discovered one thing for which we did not have a handle, after all! The wind direction and speed – which had been a huge boost for us going to Boise seemed to turn on us when we needed it most. Yes, there were alternate places to land if we decided we would not make it with the gas we had, but that meant we would lose time because unless we could first fly the timing line, our time would continue accruing. Only once during all the races did we choose to do that, and of course, it was out of necessity, but that was a much later race.

Ah, yes. The winds were chaotic all right but so far I was able to pin-point our location even as it shifted us first one way and then another – off course. We had experienced the rugged terrain on our way out but now every minute counted and I kept rechecking alternate airport locations, not wanting to think about having to land for gas except at Ogden. We reached several 'go or no go' decision points, but still we seemed to have the slenderest of margins in our favor. So, each time we continued on.

Later in '619's life with me, I would have a better feel for gas consumption. During those last stressful miles to Ogden, first I was sure we would be able to make it with no problem, but then the wind would push against us and I could feel the tanks emptying at a dizzying rate. Finally we arrived at the long line of salt flats of varying shades of blues and pinks lining up on our path into Odgen.

There was no longer a safe alternate, and as we were low in our flight path due to the winds being less at that altitude, there was no place to go but straight ahead. I was urging '619 to take us to safety when I realized I was no longer only thinking it, but saying it out loud as Brooks began the chant, too.

A whoosh of triumph and relief emanated from both Brooks and me, once we were over land again and flying max speed across the timing line. But although we were finally out of the worst of the danger, if we wanted to stay in the race (we did!) we still had to circle to land, and then make it to the pumps for gas. Brooks went out as far as she dared to make the turns as flat as possible so that whatever gas was left would not be moved outward on the tanks and starve the engine. Brooks did a great job and we were cleared to land and to taxi straight to the service area.

We both expected that at any minute the engine would stop as we were way past the amount of possible useful gas left and we knew it. Now, just how did '619 manage to do that? I was busily wondering just that very thing as the engine quit. But, pretty as you please, we rolled the rest of the way right up to the pump in silence.

Ogden tower, and what a welcome sight.

It was a good thing we were planning to spend

the night, because both sets of legs were like rubber as we walked into the service ops. We were greeted by the welcoming committee with a box of the most beautiful, dark red Bing cherries. They oozed sweet juice that dripped down our chins. I've often wondered, in retrospect, if the cherries were really as outstanding as we thought, or was life so incredibly good in those moments that the taste and experience was totally amplified.

Over breakfast we found a local pilot to ask about the pass out of Ogden the next morning. It had been a sticking point in planning between the two of us. Neither of us knew for sure that even with the morning coolness if the pass would be a problem after flying the timing line to restart the next leg. Did we need to pick another lower pass which would add to the time since it wasn't a straight shot? The pilot we spoke to assured us she did it all the time, meaning taking the pass that was in line with flying the timing line. What she neglected to say but told us later was that she always made one climbing circle before reaching the pass to get a bit more elevation. Sorry, she said, but she had just forgotten to mention it as she always just did it.

Airport is to the left and the slight dip on the right is the pass we attempted with inaccurate knowledge of the rise of elevation.

In a race you have to wait for official sunrise in order to be cleared for takeoff and to fly the timing line. We were about third in line to get clearance for take-off, having already done our run up and completing the check lists. If we had been just a matter of a few

Conga line waiting for official sunrise to take off.

minutes later there might be an early end to this story, because once the sun started warming the air, performance always dropped ever so slightly.

Brooks was one of the best instrument pilots I have flown with. The irony of that is that she was forever getting lost when she started flying. Her instructor insisted that she get her instrument ticket just as soon as she had passed her check ride for her private pilot license. That way, at least she would no longer be lost all the time. It meant that Brooks had a sure and steady hand and could hold a line and altitude with a great degree of accuracy, all of which became essential as we approached the pass.

Because of just having taken off and flown way out to get to max speed to fly the timing line, we were at full power and fully accelerated when we started our climb to go straight up to the opening in the pass. The sharp rocky outcrops grew closer as we seemingly slowly rose up the incline and I could see when we were only half way up that we were maybe going to be in trouble before we got to the top. Brooks knew that we could no longer turn away without catching a wing tip, so the only way to go was to continue up.

As if all this wasn't enough to deal with, suddenly the sun popped up through the crevice at the very top and blinded Brooks in spite of her sunglasses and the sun visor that was extended. Instantly, she went on instruments only, straining to see the gauges with all the brightness blasting her in the face. Holding a map to protect my eyes, I moved sideways enough that in spite of the sun, peripherally, I could keep track of the terrain and adjust her path verbally.

This is when '619's abilities came into play. Normally as you climb you can feel the reduction of power in the thinner and, in this case, warming air, but I swear '619 never lost one iota of her forward and upward motion. With Brooks able to hold steady on the instruments and making the minuscule corrections I gave from the visual references I had, we finally popped over the last ridge and onto a flatter plane of land for a few miles, as we made our way to Cheyenne and then Grand Island where we would recuperate for the night.

When we emerged from the plane in Grand Island I found myself hugging the wing strut of '619 and mentally thanking her for getting us through. I really was beginning to understand how absolutely special she was and how different she was from all the other planes I had flown before her. Funny to think or say you count on an inanimate object, but she was no longer merely that to me, and I found I was counting on her to be more than most thought she could be. It was comforting to have that feeling in my gut, but probably not the wisest thing as it sometimes meant I pushed the limits more than I might have without it.

We arrived in Toledo at the end of the race in the middle of the pack, just behind Pauline Glasson who had a score of 22.8354 with us at 22.6887, which is not much of a difference in 2,606 miles of racing. Our biggest win, though, was in just finishing and not being in either a toxic mess, or a pile of aluminum on the craggy peak of a mountain. The two smallest aircraft in the race were the Cessna 172s—one was Pauline's and the other was ours. Although the other planes were much faster and more powerful, there wasn't one I would have traded for '619. She was a huge winner to Brooks and to me. Sad to say that, although I didn't know it at the time, Brooks and I had just flown our last race together. I always thought there would be another one for us but it wasn't destined to be.

Competition in flying the timing line!

Chapter Six

1978 Air Race Classic   Racer #10

THE HUGHES AIRWEST
AIR RACE CLASSIC

The following June, Paul and I replaced the #22 on the tail of '619 with #10 for the second Air Race Classic. The race started in an unseemly place, Las Vegas, NV, and would run 2,584 miles in a rather zig-zag fashion to end up in Destin-Fort Walton Beach, FL. My co-pilot and now seasoned air racer was once again my daughter, Laura, who had earned, in addition to her commercial ticket (license), her single/multi engine land (not sea) with instrument rating.

In December, she expected to add her A&P (airframe and power plant) mechanics license to the list along with her CFI (Certified Flight Instructor) certificate. I had also added my instrument ticket by going to Atlanta for a week, so we felt we were much more able to contend with whatever came up. And by now we were very much aware 'something' was bound to come up...

I found a letter to Laura in the notebooks, about the trip home in '619 after getting my instrument ticket in Atlanta, and it is a story that tells me a lot of this stuff I learned, all of it that was connected to the plane, just wasn't so easy as I'd originally thought.

2-17-78

Dear Laura,

I am sitting in the airport motel in Raleigh, NC. It is 10 a.m. and the fog shrouds the building across the street. It was supposed to start clearing at 9 a.m. but you know how that goes. I am 2.7 hours from Baltimore and gas, then 1.7 to Morristown (NJ). It shouldn't be bad if I can leave but I'm not really anxious to go after yesterday's flight, which as you can readily appreciate, I will relate.

This new, shiny new, IFR pilot got her weather
briefing and filed a flight plan from ATL (Atlanta) to
RDU (Raleigh Durham) with my alternate Greensboro,
NC. All looked pretty good, maybe IFR half the way, but
1500' ceiling forecast at my destination. Some rain
freezing at level above me etc. etc.

I don't think I was ten minutes out when I was given
an altitude (Atlanta was BUSY!) that put me in the clouds
solid. – And so it remained for **3 hours!** With rain most
of the way, sometimes HARD, and the thermometer saying 32.5 degrees. I had some carburetor ice I quickly
eliminated (I was listening and watching SO CLOSELY!)
but wing ice was never a real problem, it was just that I
wasn't used to being all alone for three hours in solid
white, which lightened and darkened occasionally. I
almost chickened out and asked to go to Charlotte but
when I got there they were calling 800 feet and had five
or six holding in the pattern already waiting to land so I
decided I needed to go on. At one point when I was really fighting fatigue and a bit of concern, Center said,
"N80619 do you know you are heading SW away from
course?"

Well, that had a tendency to blow everything away,
but I said "No, I show coming up on Melia intersection."
He said, "Oh, sorry, disregard." Whew.

Finally the eyes and neck were about ready to give
up when Raleigh approach told me to report at an intersection but then said, "Disregard, we have radar
contact." I was headed 060 degrees for ILS 5 and
wouldn't you know because of my slow speed he had to
vector me through it and back, and asked me to keep
my speed to cruise as long as possible in the glide

slope. I finally said "nuts" and slowed it down properly so I could keep the needles somewhere near center. He said it was 400' and ½, (meaning the ceiling at the field was 400'and visibility half mile.) *I do not believe it was that good when I actually got to the runway.*

It wasn't raining as hard as it had once in a while but it was bad enough. When I was switched to the tower they said, "Braking action reported 'nil' by a Cherokee." This was after I had hit my MDA (minimum descent altitude) and there was NOTHING but fog. Finally after straining to see through the thick mist there was the rabbit (an approach flashing light system) and I continued descending. It was forever before I saw the width of the runway, and put her down nice and slow, and soft, and found it was very skittery but not too bad. With the warning I had been fine and '619 tiptoed oh so carefully.

I had to taxi for what seemed like forever while I searched for a turnoff, while I listened to the Bonanza bellyache he was being vectored out again as he had come too close. He said, "I knew this would happen when approach told me I was only four miles behind a CESSNA!" with distain dripping from his words. That's OK I thought, and patted her, saying "Tough luck Bonanza, we got here!" but not to anyone but '619 and myself.

In looking back I really felt proud (nasty as that is) that I had done well, and I HAD done well. I was precise and I understood everything I needed to and did not get rattled. I had not fallen apart, although I felt it wasn't far away.

By the time you get this you will know I made a reservation on United for a flight to Newark in case the fog doesn't let up here or all the way up the coast. They are saying freezing rain up here and bad, bad weather this weekend and I don't feel it is worth hanging around. We are supposed to get hit hard tomorrow and Sunday at the house too, so I'll have to return some other weekend and pick her up.

Well, that is two instrument ratings in her, and a flock of tough hours, but I sure do love her, and I will NEVER forget my first solo qualified IFR ride! But she always makes sure I get where I am going, and safely, doesn't she? I am grateful for all the good experience I have had, once more it is something no one can take from me, I had to do it myself, and of course with '619, but we did it well. For me I think this is the zest of life, I know I am alive.

Love,
    Mom

Second Annual Invitational
Air Race Classic

Las Vegas, NV to Destin-Fort Walton Beach, FL

Designated Airports on the Route	Statute Miles
1. McCarran International Airport, Las Vegas, NV	
2. Walker Field, Grand Junction, CO	419.29
3. Natrona County International, Casper, WY	283.32
4. Lee Bird Field, North Platte, NB	321.50
5. Executive Airport-Johnson County, Olathe, KS	352.97
6. Clinton Sherman Industrial Airpark, Burns Flat, OK	345.72
7. Memorial Field, Hot Springs National Park, AR	351.90
8. Gulfport-Biloxi Regional Airport, Gulfport, MS	367.50
9. Destin-Fort Walton Beach Airport, Destin, FL	141.50
TOTAL ROUTE MILEAGE (Statute Miles)	2,583.70

Paul made the trip out to Las Vegas for the start of the ARC with us in '619. After being in Las Vegas for a few days with a 24-hour, unending day, all the racers were definitely not at their best, some being in much worse shape than others. Then, the race began one fine morning with Wayne Newton bringing down the start flag for each of us. Paul discovered later that the film in the camera never advanced so we had nothing to remind us of that special moment, and I suppose it doesn't really matter in the long run. It wasn't as big a deal as the fun we had skimming the surface of the Gulf after leaving Gulfport on our way to Destin, waving *up* at the people in the cabins of big cruisers who I'm certain never, ever expected to see a fast flying plane *below* them.

Skimming over the water of the Gulf.

Rather than flying what appeared to be the shortest route over land, we had opted to take the water route for the last leg. Otherwise, we would have had to make a circuit around Pensacola NAS and their airbase, anyway, but by being lower than their radar, it was not an issue and we did not intrude in their airspace.

We almost had a catastrophe as we started to overfly what appeared to be a big floating log, which it was. But, it had about a hundred seagulls perched on it that decided to all take off just in front of us. Somehow '619 managed not to hit any of them, but I never could figure out how she managed it. I think maybe it was that we were so much faster than their lift-off, that they and we were spared the collision. It could have been bad as there was no recovery time built into the situation, and we would undoubtedly have crashed without enough altitude, and *that* we definitely did not have.

2—The Daily Advance   Tuesday, June 27, 1978

nation

OLATHE, Kan. — Two contestants were seriously hurt Monday in a plane crash during a cross-country airplane race for women pilots. Dorothy Birdsong, Temple Terrace, Fla., and Ethel Gibson, St. Petersburg, Fla., crashed as they approached the Johnson County Airport near here. Seventy-nine women pilots left Las Vegas Saturday in the second annual Air Race Classic and were scheduled to reach Destin-Ft. Walton, Fla., today.

It was all a bit stressful. The heat and humidity added to the stress, as keeping the wheels in their shiny wheel pants up and out of the briny water took constant but light pressure on the yoke. But, still, one couldn't have too much, in order to maintain the fastest attitude of the plane. For optimum speed we had to stay within a wing length of the brilliant, soft blue water which wouldn't have been soft if we had hit it. Trying to ignore dolphins playing was otherwise the only thing I found to break up the monotony of flying across but so close to the water, for the hours it took to the end of the race.

After we flew the timing line in Destin, it took a while to get out of the plane after landing. It seemed my hands were curled so tight around the yoke it was like they were welded onto it. Several hours later after dinner, a relaxing dip in the pool and some alcoholic libation my hands finally started to uncurl. But it was a time for great celebration as we discovered we were well within the top third of the racers, and once again the first of the smaller, slower aircraft.

Releasing the tension and stress with silliness. Merri, another contestant (with the lettuce on her head) and Brooks ,who had come to the finish of the race in her favorite charter plane.

Brooks in '22Y arriving at Destin.

Brooks' favorite plane, '22Y

Also to make it even sweeter we were some nine places ahead of the plane that was our direct competition, my dear friend, Pauline Glasson. Our water race leg that caused so much physical stress was what had made the big difference, and suddenly it was worth it all. We also came in third fastest on that leg which was saying a great deal when one considered the other planes and equipment we were flying against. The slower planes, although handicapped, seemed to have much more time to make crucial mistakes, or to wear their pilots out.

Start of the race introductions at the banquet.

Laura and Kay with the #10 race number and sponsors stars at the Vegas start.

Showing a sponsor where his star was located.

Pictures taken when flying on races are never great photographs because of the Plexiglas and reflections, the movement of the aircraft and the fact that one is dealing with vibrations. Also there is only time to take them when things are quiet and the photos one really would like during the bad stuff are never possible because you are way too busy! Also the turbulence creates its own difficulties. So apologies, and many of the slides scanned were more than thirty or so years old and had not been stored in a climate controlled environment. The quality deteriorated somewhat, but they tell a story when mere words cannot begin to do justice to the scene.

These are just some of the unique landscapes near Vegas.

There are unique things that have to be solved when flying small planes. Figuring out the weather for instance, and having an alternate plan of action. You can end up in places you never expected to find yourself. This can be an entirely new adventure if you let it.

When a storm front rolls in across your intended path there *are* options, that is – if you cannot avoid it, go over it or go around it. Underneath is not usually a good option with hail and/or destructive winds probable. As Laura and I headed out to the start of the race we were nearing Pecos, Texas, what I might at that time have called a one horse town. Actually, when we landed, we found a charming if tiny zoo with pretty zebras, which made it more than just a one-horse town. It was a good time to take pictures as the sun behind the storm front headed earthward for the night.

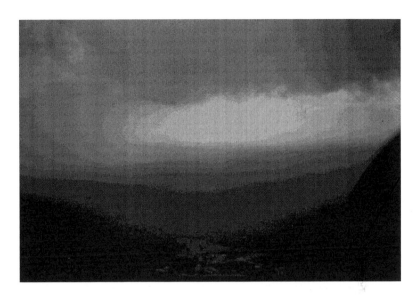

Laura watching the rain and storm clouds coming in at the little zoo with the zebra.

Another strange thing about stopping in unexpected places is that you have no clue if there will be a place to lay your body down, and if there is – can you actually get to it? Pecos had one motel, situated out on the Interstate, which was the town's main thoroughfare. The only person around the airport office volunteered to get us there. No problem, he said about us getting a room, they were never full.

We grabbed our emergency rations and our clothes and went off to check in after being sure '619 was well tied down in case of wind. It looked like we had the only occupied room, but if we could get a good night's sleep we would not complain. No one knew us or knew we were even there, so we anticipated a peaceful night.

Just after the late summer sunset we were getting ready to climb in bed and make an early night to balance an early morning getting up, when suddenly there was a hearty and loud banging on the door. Laura and I just looked at each other. What to do? Should we answer, being two women alone in a strange place? But what if it was a fire and they just wanted us out safely! I threw on a shirt and went to the door intending to crack it just a bit, when it went WHAM! blasting back into the wall behind me. I suddenly found myself in an immense bear hug being lifted off the ground by a man I had never seen before in my life!

Laura was heading over to protect me, when I was set down on the floor again and the stranger pronounced, "Well, I am A. G. Blevins, and you must be kin!!!"

While I got my breath he proceeded to tell us he was the local agriculture pilot and had just finished his last run of spraying fertilizer. When he landed, he saw our plane with our names and race numbers tied down in the transient parking, and knew he had to come and visit us. He knew where he would find us. He then insisted we get dressed so he could take us to dinner – in the only place open to get food – and of course they knew him and would fix us all right up.

Because he was a force to be reckoned with we found ourselves dressed and while eating, we filled him in on our journey while we traded histories. Or, at least, what I knew of the Blevins clan coming from England to settle in the corner of North Carolina, Tennessee and Virginia, as well as Paul's father's family. And that is how I came to know that any Blevins, *all Blevins*, are kin in some way or fashion. How A. G. got way out in Pecos I do not remember but there must not be a lot of Blevins out there in that lonely part of the state. However, he was absolutely delightful! And, indeed, he must be kin!

Kay's son Tom, putting all the decals on. This is what AG Blevins saw when he landed and knew we must be kin.

107

Rarely have I landed at a small airport without feeling comfortable and the recipient of loads of local hospitality. I have been handed keys to cars with no concern at all, fed homemade meals and of course, the essential element at an airport, always given a cup of coffee. It might be awful depending on the time of day, but the friendliness with which it is offered makes it taste pretty good.

Another unique thing about flying small planes is the fact that along with weather you have to reckon with other logistics, such as the realization that the human body with several cups of the morning liquid, be it coffee or tea, *WILL* have to make a pit stop sooner or later. '619 was equipped with long range fuel tanks and unless I was very cautious with liquid intake, the plane could go longer distances on its fuel, than I could hold that fine airport coffee. On the longer trips we tended to even take a thermos full of the 'keep awake and alert' stuff of the gods.

Frequently the flight plan needed to be longer than I would have liked, but then we had in the airplane the equivalent to the men's long necked but lidded plastic bottles they used – mostly without incident, being tucked away from prying eyes to be emptied at the next airport lounge. I have received unusual gifts through the years, such as a 'step-check' – a 3-legged folding stool- type step, that I could perch on to check fuel in the high wing. That was an especially great gift and great help for someone as height-challenged as myself. I used it every flight.

Another really handy, dandy gift (I think it was for Mother's Day) was my very own Jill-John. It is exactly what you might be thinking, except you wonder, just how would something like that work? Well, let me tell you. It does leave something to be desired – but in an emergency, it is a true blessing.

When I was presented with the gift it rather looked like a woman's cosmetic travel case or a plastic container for curlers or the like. On opening I discovered a long plastic tube that was attached to a pretty good sized heavy duty plastic bag that looked rather impervious, something that would hold up really well. But the other end of the tubing was affixed to a softer plastic or rubber like cup rather like the size of a small half grapefruit. I was supposed to do what with it??

It wasn't too difficult to figure out what to do with it, but my imagination took off in spite of seeing the practicality. You can believe that I was in no hurry to use it. It was given a place of honor, where it could actually be easily reached if necessary, but I never really thought I would have to use it.

Frequently when flying a charter, my uniform would be a proper lady's suit, nylons, and heels, for in those years, that was what a professional pilot wore. Many clients seemed to be reassured with the appearance, since they sometimes had difficulties enough in adjusting to having a female pilot.

And then the day came. I was in uniform but had not yet picked up my passenger. I believe I was heading west from New York to Lexington, Kentucky. Because of a bit of iffy weather midway and being a wee bit short of time, I had filed an IFR flight plan (Instrument Flight Rules). This meant I was flying through quite a busy corridor, being handed off from one traffic control area to the next and all were busy to their max. Somewhere approaching Harrisburg, Pennsylvania that second cup of coffee an old friend had insisted I have with him before leaving, started being quite insistent. It starts as that first little niggling feeling that this needs to be attended to pretty soon, then after some wiggling in the seat, I think oh, it will be OK. But as the radio chatter to and from me to the Center becomes more intense, so does the feeling that no way am I going to make it to the airport! Surely that is what the Jill-John is for – an emergency! And this feeling is rapidly escalating into an emergency.

Then Control announced they have just had an emergency and will have to reroute me. I did not reply that I was having my own emergency, but instead repeated back to him the instructions, changing my heading as I reached for the innocuous looking 'cosmetic case' stashed just behind the front seats. It was at this point I ran into the 'iffy weather' that announced itself with excessive turbulence and getting the latch on the flap to open was a challenge in itself. I wished I had tried to use it sometime earlier in less demanding circumstances.

Finally, I got the box open, and used the co-pilot seat as a bench to organize everything. There really wasn't much to it. I just had to get my skirt out of the way, my panty hose down to my knees and the underpants out of the way too. With the increasing turbulence, it was proving to be quite a feat to hang onto the yoke, talk to Center, make the clothes adjustment, keep my altitude and heading, put the grapefruity thing under me trying not to leak onto the seat and then convince myself it was really OK to let loose.

Somewhere in the chaos I started to giggle. I cannot giggle just a little bit. Once it starts it always seems to escalate. And that is, of course, when I missed answering the radio. After finally getting everything in position, I could not convince that recalcitrant or rebellious part of me that was being so hesitant that it really was alright to let go! I realized my altitude was slipping and then I heard my call sign asking me if I could 'read control' which meant I hadn't answered before, and he was wondering if my radios were working. I was still giggling when I finally answered, and he came back with "'619 confirm you are one soul on board". Heck, yes, I was the only soul on board, or I wouldn't be going through all this, but what to answer him so he no longer thought I was a nut case?

"'619 has only one soul on board," I replied, "but that soul is having trouble with turbulence and a Jill-John. Sorry for the delay."

"Confirmed, '619, I can clear you back to your original course." And he transferred me to the next area control. That did not mean that everything else was under control, but it was slowly but surely getting handled and about that time the turbulence seemed to slack off a bit and I could get the little box with its hidden treasure closed up, so it wouldn't spill all over the cockpit. The pantyhose didn't get pulled back up until I had shut the engine down after landing. I did have a lot of adjustments to my suit before I could leave the cockpit but I stepped down with my little cosmetic case and daintily walked into flight ops as if nothing was out of the ordinary. Except I found I was still giggling.

Kay opening her present of the Jill-John. You have no idea of what she is thinking either!!

Chapter Seven

1979 Angel Derby, Recreation of 1929 Air Race
Racer #1

The next year brought the race of all races. We
heard about this special race that was being planned
and it seemed to be exactly the right kind of race for
our slower, less powerful plane. It was a repeat of an
Angel Derby flown by early women aviator notables
such as Amelia Earhart and Louise Thaden. In fact, this
race was to be an actual duplication of a race route of
fifty years before, flown in 1929.

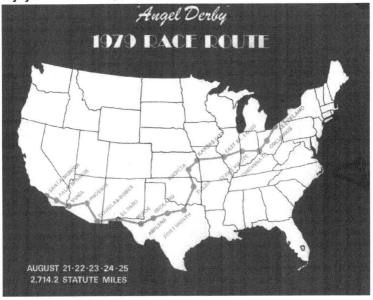

Obviously these routes and legs were designed
for the aircraft of that day, not the twins and high performance singles that we had been competing against
recently. The race legs were short and there were

many race stops so the faster planes hardly had time to get to their optimum altitude before they had to pull the plug and descend. It seemed we hardly ever had time to get to our best high altitude whenever we raced, so we chose lower altitudes most of the time. Time versus distance was a key factor.

ALL WOMEN'S INTERNATIONAL AIR RACE, INC.

FIRST WOMEN'S AIR DERBY

50th ANNIVERSARY

COMMEMORATIVE RACE

SCHEDULE

```
IMPOUND OPENS, Clover Field, Santa Monica, CA . . . 0900 PDT, August 17, 1979
IMPOUND CLOSES  . . . . . . . . . . . . . . . . . . 1700 PDT, August 18, 1979
INSPECTIONS CLOSE . . . . . . . . . . . . . . . . . 1700 PDT, August 19, 1979
RACE BRIEFINGS  . . . . . . . . . . . . . . . . . . 0900 PDT, August 20, 1979
TAKEOFF . . . . . . . . . . . . . . . . . . . . . . 0900 PDT, August 21, 1979
MANDATORY PREFINISH DEADLINE, Columbus . . . . . . . 1900 EDT, August 24, 1979
FINISH, Cleveland . . . . . . . . . . . . . . . . . 1400 EDT, August 25, 1979
AWARDS BANQUET  . . . . . . . . . . . . . . . . . . 2000 EDT, August 28, 1979
```

DESIGNATED ROUTE AND AIRPORTS

		Statute Miles
1.	Clover Field, Santa Monica, CA	
**2.	Palm Springs Airport, CA	112.6
***3.	Yuma International Airport, AZ	136.5
***4.	Phoenix Deer Valley Airport, AZ	162.6
***5.	Bisbee-Douglas International Airport, AZ	210.6
***6.	El Paso International Airport, TX	191.2
***7.	Pecos Municipal Airport, TX	172.3
***8.	Midland Regional Airport, TX	85.9
***9.	Abilene Municipal Airport, TX	151.3
***10.	Meacham Field, Fort Worth, TX	138.4
***11.	Tulsa International Airport, OK	247.8
***12.	Wichita Mid-Continent Airport, KS	131.7
***13.	Fairfax Airport, Kansas City, KS	195.0
***14.	Bi-State Park Airport, East St. Louis, IL	243.1
***15.	Hulman Field, Terre Haute, IN	165.2
***16.	Lunken Field, Cincinnati, OH	156.7
*17.	Port Columbus Airport, OH	102.6
18.	Burke-Lakefront Airport, Cleveland, OH	126.6
	TOTAL MILES	2716.1

```
***Must Flyby, Designated refueling airport
**Must Flyby, emergency stopping only
*Must Stop and remain overnight, group takeoff for finish leg.
```

In my notebook I found notes from AVMETS, a weather consulting firm, about how to determine the best outcome or how to plan a race. If you have no interest in knowing about that part of racing you have my permission to skip the next italicized portions.

Selection of Routes

All routes will be minimum *AIR DISTANCE ROUTES* which in most all cases will not be Great Circle routes due to the winds. This is the Least Time Track method of flying pressure pattern.

Check Points

Check points may be VOR's, Cities, Towns, Airports and in most cases will be a combination of all of the above. We will assume that the tract between each check point is a great circle which is approximately a straight line on a Lambert Chart. If the check point should be an airport, town or city then we will assume that you should pass over the center of same.

Plotting your route

From the race flight plan (which will be given via phone) draw straight lines between each check point on your sectional chart. Then enter the forecast times at each check point. In addition, enter 10 min time marks on your route between check points. (10 min times GS [ground speed] for that area equals distance flown.)

When Airborne

Enter off time then your ETA's (estimated time of arrival) for each check point as well as the ETA's for the 10 min time marks.

Enroute

Fly your forecast CH (course heading) and with pencil on the map, eye outside and on the clock, there is no reason to be more than a mile or two off track at any time. When you find yourself either right or left of *desired track correct a few degrees to slowly come back to desired track. Some of the reasons of being off track are: Not flying the CH properly, Drift more/less than forecast, Compass error and not applying the compass Dev. for your aircraft to the CH provided by Avmets. Our CH assumes zero Deviation.*

# # #

I also found in my notebook a copy of this letter from which I have taken an excerpt that will be explained later:

February 13, 1980
To Mr. Glen Nickerman, President, GH Aircraft, El Monte, CA
In the long winter months, especially in NJ, one finds time to pause and reflect on all the good things that occurred in the last summer and to savor the best.
The good help and warm reception that Laura and I received at your service operation the fateful day during the first leg of the Angel Derby when our engine lost power, has been a many times told story across this country of ours. Sister racers and fellow East Coast pilots have had your praises sung to them when they asked how we did in the Anniversary Angel Derby.

Ahhh, so why did we require help from El Monte Airport when that was NOT on our race route? It all started when Laura and I drew the #1 position in the race. Because of that and because the start of the race called for us to depart after flying the timing line and continue flying seaward out to circle around the Santa Monica pier before reversing course and heading

east, we huddled prior to departure with the twin en-
gined and faster pilots that were in place following us.

Agreement was reached that we would stay as
low and close to the pier as possible and they would
fly above and around us, as at their accelerated speed
they would run us down if we did not let them know
exactly where we would be.

Having arrived at the last possible minute in Santa
Monica due to fog with all the Eastern pilots on our
tail, it meant that Laura could not be in attendance for
our last minute maintenance as planned. She was required to be in the mandatory pilot briefing with me,
and no one could check on the overburdened maintenance people trying to handle the great numbers
who needed their oil changed and plugs swapped
out. That fact alone started a chain of events never to
be forgotten.

The flag drop for us, in first position, to start the race.

The Los Angeles basin is noted for smog, fog and poor visibility. Add in the huge number of planes flying in and out of the various large and small airports in that same area, plus we were not really familiar with any of it. We were as prepared as possible, and our biggest concern was to stay out of the way of the racers behind us.

The flag came down and as #1 we excitedly pushed the throttle to the wall, leapt from the runway and raced for the pier turning right as sharply as possible around it, not seeing the beautiful ocean but watching our altitude and distances, knowing we must stay above minimums but below traffic. We were being thankful that everything was good so far. Just about the time I made a comment that we were crossing downtown Los Angeles, judging by the buildings below us, going from 800 feet to 1400 feet, our world suddenly tilted with a big bang.

There was a great loud noise and equally great vibration that shook us like a toy in a dog's mouth, and then in shock we realized the engine had stopped. Here we were, over downtown Los Angeles on a Friday morning, with all roads full to capacity and the smog so thick we could not see much of any distance to even try to find a place to land. Laura said immediately, "Hang a left." I did so. She then said, "You have two options, find a roof top with as few mechanicals and air conditioning units as possible, or, if you continue north on this course and can see the river, then there is an airport to the east of the river. I do not know if you can make it, though."

This is the moment when you have to really trust. Trust your gut, some say; others say trust God, but I think both those were absolutely necessary, and then even more importantly could '619 do the impossible and make it to that airport? By now I trusted '619, so I told Laura I was going for the airport. Checking roof tops became secondary, as I set up for the best glide angle I could, putting all our eggs in the one basket, the aluminum tube of '619.

Pilots always train for emergencies. Pilots are always aware of having someplace mapped out or a distant field seen from the far corner of the eye, that would be the place to put down if the engine quit. It is always, or should be, running at all times just in the forefront of the background of your mind. You should always be ready. But you always wonder how you will do if it happens to you. Not so much if as when. You are always aware of the possibility, or should be if you want to survive a calamity.

Since we were at a lower altitude than normal to start with because of the racers following, there wasn't a whole lot of space between us and hard earth below us. Other than the loud noises and tremendous vibrations we had experienced and the quiet since then, we really were not sure of what might have happened. Yes, we tried to restart the engine even though it felt like a futile action, but nothing changed.

We re-tightened our seat belts after checking to make sure there were no loose items that could become projectiles, and ran through a verbal checklist to be sure we would be ready when the plane met the ground. No, there wasn't much we could do in the situation. We were going down. Laura contacted El Monte Airport and apprised them of the situation, telling them that we were trying for a landing at their field, so if we made it that far they would be ready and authorize a straight in landing.

That glide was really short in duration but it seemed to take forever. Finally we spotted the river with relief, and then Runway 1 was actually in sight just past Interstate 10 but with many various kinds of buildings in between. We kept the glide just on the edge, hanging by our fingertips so to speak, and then finally with a satisfying bump our wheels touched the very end of the runway and rolled beyond. We continued rolling, no power, and carefully turned off the first taxiway on the right, finally coming to a stop out of the way of other traffic.

One small in-breath of relief, and then Laura was out the door, unlocking the cowling and propping it up so she could see what was going on. Laura had completed her Airframe and Powerplant certification at Western Michigan so she was now a certified mechanic and that is what we needed right now.

What I find in looking back is that it was an unspoken agreement that if we could fix it we would get back in the race. Forget that we were lucky to have our lives and did not crash, and thinking we had a chance to continue on was ludicrous. But Laura quickly found two problems which had been the probable cause of our dilemma.

She pointed out to me as the airport support team arrived at our side, that one spark plug was cross-threaded into the cylinder. She had already been to the baggage bay and had the spare spark plugs in hand and quickly pulled out all the ones in use and replaced them. I do not remember who saw that several of those she pulled were cracked, and commented that it looked like they had been dropped, maybe had rolled off the mechanic's bench, but cracked they definitely were. It is no wonder that '619 had an engine failure, but quite remarkable that we made it safely to an airport.

More plane hugs! I hate to think of the results if that catastrophe had happened on a full power take off and turn around the pier, as I do not think '619 knew how to swim.

With everyone watching Laura, I got back in the cockpit and when she motioned to me, I tried to restart the engine. Miracles do happen. '619 roared into action as if there had never been a hitch. Laura stowed the tools, we thanked the crew that had given us cold drinks and good wishes, and did a very careful perusal of the check list and listened alertly to the engine run-up. Laura called the tower and we taxied out to continue on our way to Palm Springs, a bit late but better late than the never we had almost experienced.

We flew the timing line at Palm Springs but did not stop to get fuel. Our long range tanks were a plus for us on this race as it meant we might be able to do that at several of the mandatory flybys. Our course to Palm Springs led us through the Los Angeles corridor and Banning Pass. We were staying low because of the steady head wind we experienced which all by itself made us feel a bit vulnerable.

I began to sense more than feel a new vibration that I had never been aware of before, and eventually Laura confirmed that she felt it too. '619 was trying to tell us that all was not quite right. In spite of that we chose to stay low over the Salton Sea, a shallow, saline rift lake located directly on the San Andreas Fault, and it was not a place you would chose to go down in. We made good time flying from five to ten feet above the lake, but I discovered the vibration became more definite and threatening during that stretch, reminding us there was not much gliding room built into flying that low.

We finally arrived in Yuma, grateful for no further loss of power. The few racers still there were surprised to see us coming in behind them since we had taken off first. While getting gas we filled in the race committee about the problem and the evidence of the spark plugs. They reminded us that our time 'off course' was still counted in our leg time and we agreed we knew that to be the case but were going to continue on and see how much time we could make up. After all this was supposed to be our race, as the airplanes of the 1920's were more like our Cessna than the fast twins running ahead of us.

Laura explaining the plug situation to the race committee in Yuma, AZ after arriving so late.

Warm welcome in Yuma!

We had reservations for the night at Deer Valley Airport north of Phoenix and there was still enough time for us to make it before sunset when all racing ceased. Our flight path to Deer Valley had a slight detour to keep us from intruding on a military area, but the very pointed rocks we crossed over had us holding our breath because there was no place to land, only a place to crash on some very solid vertical rock. Just as we had mostly cleared the pointy terrain, '619 had seemingly waited until that occurred, and there was loud and noisy engine commotion and the propeller just wind-milled once again without power.

Laura had it handled once again, as she picked up the mike and called Litchfield city airport tower. We soon found out that Goodyear, the name of the airport, was the training base for Lufthansa pilots, and there appeared to be a large number of yellow bees circling the airport, as all the training planes sported a coat of yellow paint.

When Laura requested a straight in, against traffic, an instant alert went up and even before the tower had an opportunity to respond to her, all the little yellow bees started moving away from the airport in quick time. The tower, with her unusual request, responded and asked if she was declaring an emergency. Understand, it is unusual enough to have a request for straight in with a busy airport, but this was a female voice, and very Southern sounding to boot, and at that point in time there were only two percent female commercial pilots.

Her very clear answer was, "Not yet." And with that, since all the traffic was pretty much gone, he cleared us to land. The air was so clear we could see forever and had no problem with seeing the airport, unlike Los Angeles. So we set up the glide angle once again, after all we were now old hands at knowing how much was too much or too little, and once again we floated down to touch the end of Runway 3, rolling to the first taxiway, turning, and rolling off a short ways to a stop.

This time though, instead of a small airport crew coming to meet us, we looked up to see two foam trucks with men in fireproof suits so hot the sweat dripped out the bottom of their long thick pants; an ambulance; an aircraft tow vehicle; trucks of all kinds, and about thirty men located at different areas next to the runway. Talk about a reception! And best of all there was no paperwork to be done since we had not actually declared an emergency.

While '619 was being towed off to the Cessna Dealer service hangar, we were treated like princesses and taken to be cooled with iced drinks and offerings of food, and anything else we thought we might like. We had definitely made life interesting for a time that day in the humdrum hours of training that usually took place on the airport. There were also

Looking back from Goodyear at the 'pointy' mountain peaks we had just crossed before the engine quit.

Getting a look at the engine in Goodyear Airport, first tear down.

offers to take us to a place to spend the night and we took the easiest one, stopping first to gather our belongings from the plane.

After calling Paul and Jack we took time to use the phone to call an old sailing buddy, Charlie Jackson, as he lived fairly close by in Wickenburg, which was about an hour north-northwest of the airport.

In the morning the engine mechanic tore down '619 to the point he could see some of the damage done by our violent shut downs. And although he thought he could remedy the situation, but with time to order parts, cylinder work and reconstruction, we had best plan on spending part to most of a week before completion. We hoped he would be kind to '619, but I know he thought she was just another Cessna.

Good sport and kind man that Charlie was, he arrived later that next morning ready to take us back to his ranch in Wickenburg. Little did we know how great that would be, and that his wife Ruth would not seem to mind at all. Ruth knew me a little from my sailing with Charlie, but only when the 28' Viking was tied up in port, as she had never participated in any of the sailing that I had done as crew with Charlie. Laura and I were introduced to the dogs and horses, but while Charlie did his horse training, we mostly spent our hours in his lovely pool.

In the meantime I was back on the phone to both Paul and Jack my friend and mechanic at home. Jack was ready to fly out to Santa Monica and throttle the mechanics in Santa Monica for causing such a serious situation by their carelessness. Paul talked several times to the owners of the service operation but they refused to get upset about any of it.

They offered to send a new set of spark plugs to make him whole, but that just added fuel to the fire, adding grave insult to the injury. In consulting with an attorney he was told that there really wasn't any recourse: that yes, he could sue them but each time Paul

Charlie waiting to load our gear and take us to the ranch.

Not exactly what you'd expect to see in Michigan – or North Carolna, either!

would go out to California for the trial they would just get a postponement until finally, Paul gave up. It would cost him mightily and he most likely would never get satisfaction from anyone.

127

Relaxing in Charlie's pool.

Jack did what he could do as an IA (a mechanic with FAA Inspection Authority) and filled in the FAA about the situation, and the fact he has a sterling reputation with the FAA it might have carried some weight. We have no idea if it made any difference or not. All I could do was tell Jack I would bring the baby home for him to make better, because I did not think the work being done at Goodyear Airport was going to solve the problem. All I wanted them to do locally was to make it possible for me to fly home safely. And then give her to Jack, who I knew could fix up '619 like new.

While Laura and I floated in Charlie's pool look-ing up into the sky in which you could see forever, we talked about how the race ended for us and how dis-appointing it was to have been scratched from a race that was a natural for us.

We also talked about how '619 had held off catas-trophe until we could safely glide to a landing, twice. She didn't quit over the ocean, or over the mountain peaks. And she made the impossible glide to El Mon-te Airport without letting us down. She didn't quit over the Salton Sea either, when it was so obvious we would go down into the brine if the engine faltered.

When we landed at Goodyear, I hadn't been able to give her the plane hugs I did so often, but my thoughts stayed with her all the while we were relax-ing at Charlie's.

About three days later we got the call to go and test fly the repairs. Charlie took us back and it was with confidence we fired her up and took off. In case you think we were not being cautious, consider that it was decided to go no further than four miles away from the airport and to circle around 3500' and make sure the engine would not repeat the problem.

I don't think that twenty minutes passed before the same old problem cropped up and the call was made to the tower that '619 was returning without power. Again the question, "Are you declaring an emergency?" and the answer "No, don't think there will be a problem getting to the runway. You don't need to send out the foam trucks or anything. Maybe the tow vehicle but that is all."

Charlie had waited for us to complete the test flight. When he heard the tower say '619 was returning, he opened the trunk of the car and put our luggage back in. After consulting with the mechanic once again, we began the ride to our extended vacation at the ranch. Charlie and Ruth were really welcoming and made it seem that they were pleased we would be continuing our stay.

Back to the pool where we became like prunes, and from there we would go down to watch the horses go through their training paces. Ruth took us in to Wickenburg to buy our obligatory cowboy hats, trying to keep us from getting more sunburned than we already were. Over the years of sitting in an unprotected cockpit, skin cancer seems to be a constant in my life now. The hats were a bit too wide to use in the cockpit though, but for hanging on the corral fence they were just right. They were wonderfully lazy peaceful days spent with Charlie and Ruth.

Eventually, after many calls to advise us of the continual additional costs that were accruing, '619 was declared to be good to go. Charlie took us back and this time we loaded up, intending to be on our way. We did circle over the airport for a while, but now we were anxious to get back to our lives in the real world.

'619 seemed to be wanting to leave too, and so we headed for Atlanta to drop Laura off at the airport where she did her flight instructing. I was familiar with Peachtree DeKalb, because I had taken my instrument and then later my certified flight instructor rating requirements. It was sort of a second home.

But there was something still amiss with '619. I kept willing her to get us home and she did just that. Yet the tension I felt was underlying everything. Trying to pinpoint what I was sensing from her as we made our way, I decided that there was some very slight vibration that I could feel through my feet, and if one was not as familiar with her normal operating vibes as I was, they would never have recognized it for what it was. And what it was, was scary.

With great relief the weather did not pose a problem and I arrived in NJ at my Flanders Valley home base many days later than expected but safe. Jack was poised ready to tear the engine down. I knew he would find whatever was still wrong with '619, and like a CSI investigator he would search for that all elusive vibration that I could feel in my feet.

The first thing he found was that '619 had served above and beyond the call of duty. It was a miracle that she had not quit on us on the trip from Litchfield, AZ to home. Now, I was given all the technical terms for what the damage that caused the major failure was, but here is a much simplified version.

Of course the start of it all was the plug that was cross threaded into the engine cylinder. That alone would have been a major problem. But add to it the several cracked spark plugs and you automatically have a recipe for disaster, considering that the engine has to develop power and those are basic ingredients in the process. Jack confirmed what Laura had discovered when she opened the cowl at El Monte Airport.

His further report had an interesting piece that helped me understand that slight vibration I felt in my feet. He said something about the intake valve, that it had warped with the heat and explosive nature of the shut downs and once in a while it would rotate and in effect be in a position to seize. Well, that certainly sounded to me as though '619 had come through yet again, I like to think, with my safety in mind and performed above and beyond the service manual's expectations of possibility. The long trip from Arizona was done as they say, 'on a wing and a prayer', but we had made it without the need to make another emergency landing. And THAT, my friend, was such a blessing.

Chapter Eight

While Jack was getting my bird back into action, my life was once again full of exciting events. For the past year, I had been working with Cessna as an East Coast Zone Administrator, but recently, there had been a change of leadership in the East Coast Zone.

The new manager took it upon himself to hire as *my* secretary someone with a sexy demeanor but absolutely no skills. In fact, she couldn't even type! I hoped Cessna would come to their senses about this new Manager, and eventually they did, but I didn't wait around for it.

The new position I hired into was with Edo-Aire, the Float plane people, where I was not only the first woman to be National Marketing Administrator but also the first person in that position not to have an engineering degree. But I was a pilot and understood aircraft avionics which was also a large part of their business. Also, I knew how to reorganize the handling of sales, integrating all the data, etc., into computer programs that worked for everyone, not just a selected few. There was one clause that pleased me greatly in the hiring agreement. It specified that if I was able to straighten out the administration of the sales operations, then I would eventually be a candidate for field sales – which is really where I wanted to be.

Doing shows was old hat to me, as we had participated in a great variety of them while at Cessna and other companies, so there wasn't much difference in doing them as a representative of Edo-Aire. I had been involved with aviation for so many years that I was longing for the opportunity to create something new and different, but there wasn't much room for that, as I continued waiting for a sales area to open up.

And suddenly there it was! Even more amazing was that it was within driving distance of my home. This meant the logistics of being married in one place and working in another wasn't even an issue. My boss called me into his office, and I was expectantly waiting to hear of my new position, when he instead told me to put an ad in the paper for the position!

No, I did not go ballistic.

I simply asked what happened to the agreement we'd signed when I was hired. He acted completely surprised! He said, "Oh, but I can't do without you in your current position. Why, there isn't anyone else who can do it." My answer was one he did not like, as he was rather fond of his secretary and her care of him, but that didn't matter to me. I told him I knew she could do it and would love to have the opportunity.

His spluttering would have almost been funny had I not been so pissed. I continued enumerating the reasons why I wanted the new position, but all he could say was, "Well, I can't put a female in the field, they can't sell. And I really can't let you go."

My answer was, "You already have."

His secretary did indeed make a wonderful Administrator and I am happy to say I was the one who helped her get started on her private pilot's license, but for her satisfaction, not theirs. She was not ever an engineer, either, but she really didn't need to be. Still, up to that time, aviation was pretty much a man's world and we women simply had to live in it. This meant we had to find our own way, in spite of the obstacles they established everywhere!

# # #

I wasn't at all sure of what to do now. I still needed to support '619, and there were all those unexpected repairs for which I had to pay Jack. Those blasted words, 'females can't sell' would not stop running around my head. After carefully examining all my options, – those in aviation and out of it – the most appealing was for an automotive sales position with Volkswagen.

Because Paul worked for General Motors in one of their Zone Offices, he felt it would be unfair for me to work for a GM dealer. Suppose I should come home some night with what I considered to be a perfectly innocent comment that would expose a bit of wrongdoing to someone of his experience. He would have no choice but to address it, and possibly cause repercussions. But there were no constraints if I should choose to work for a different car company.

Once again I ran into a situation where the owner of the dealership wasn't sure females could sell cars. What was this bias I kept running into? Women of today should thank all of us who stuck our necks out, and took the bashing we did, so they would have it easier! In the end, however, he did hire me, saying 'even though you drive a Corvette.'

In spite of those words, I detected a bit of admiration, especially when, in answer to his query, I explained that the license plate of "K FLIES" was given to me by my co-workers at Avionics Products to honor my racing. But that was after I was hired.

To be sure, the men in the sales department could be heard scoffing and making snide comments about a woman in sales. Outwardly, at least, the sales manager was polite as he laid out the rules of the showroom, but with very few helpful hints or real aids to selling cars. I was simply put into the rotation for the 'ups' and soon it was my turn to meet and greet the customer walking in the door.

It was the mailman!

There was a snicker from the desk behind me, but I got up and met the mailman as he dropped the mail in the office. After introducing myself, we chatted quietly, and I discovered that no one had ever asked him if he was interested in buying a car. And then I realized that the other salespeople had suddenly sprouted ears like Dumbo!

He told me he'd always wanted a Vanagon, or camper, and there was one sitting in the middle of the showroom floor. I had never been in one myself, either, but with confidence I led him to it, and together we started exploring the vehicle. Since I knew nothing at all about writing up a contract I asked the Sales Manager for help and he kindly obliged. Heck, I didn't even know what the price should be, but the man wanted one, so I found that out, too.

After that episode, whenever I asked for materials to learn about the various models, I was given everything I wanted. Of course, I made it a point to ask questions at every turn and also made myself well-known in the shop, as well. I wanted to know the opinions of the mechanics about all sorts of things. Soon, I was not a bother to them, but rather a welcome audience, one to whom they could happily show off their knowledge.

Many of the salesmen thought it was a fluke, when I was the top salesperson in the second month I was there. But I was only doing what they said to do! I made cold calls on the phone whenever I had time, and I diligently followed up on any lead or referral given to me. Pretty soon I had won the title of best sales person for the month – for three months in a row – and I discovered I had inadvertently knocked off the leader board one of the long-time best salesmen in the tri-state region.

He was intrigued by this, and frequently I would find him at my desk asking questions of me. His sales had remained steady, so he wasn't hurting, because after all, I had developed business no one else seemed to want. It was very obvious to everyone that I was enjoying it all very much. Interestingly, in the years that followed, that salesman continued calling me from time to time, just to see what I was doing and what was happening. When I left he regained his standing back once again.

The dealer sent me to two Volkswagen schools thinking it would be a good investment. At least I think that was his reasoning, but I greatly enjoyed the realization that the concept of how to sell was something I already seemed to know. That is not bragging.

I just always knew that 'administration' duties were not what made me happy. But sales? Well, that just seemed to come naturally to me, and there was a great deal of joy in being able to satisfy a customer's desire. At that time, it simply seemed the best and easiest way to continue paying the bills for '619.

Eat your heart out, Edo-Aire. Didn't you know women can't sell? Can't fly either, according to some. But we know better, don't we?

# # #

There is no way to know how long I might have continued selling a brand of car that was not our primary source of income. Because of the social activities with the dealers in Paul's area, I was hardly a stranger to many of the General Motors dealers. It didn't take long for the word to get out that I was selling VW's, and that did not seem to be a problem by itself. But when my success became known, too, some of those dealers thought I was undermining their sales.

Then Paul began to hear about it. The more I sold the more he heard. He never asked me to quit, but I became aware of the pressure it was creating. Finally at a cocktail party, one of his dealers asked me point blank, "When are you going to stop?"

So I turned back to the aviation community to see what might be available and that would generate enough income so I could pay all the expenses of '619's upkeep. Jack had been wonderful about not charging what he should have for the engine rebuild. It was still a huge out-of-pocket expense we hadn't anticipated! And then there was the gas. If I wanted to fly, I needed to be able to pay for the gas.

As I had been based at Morristown Airport in NJ with Cessna, I started my search with the people I knew from there. I was offered a part-time flight- and ground-school instructor position at Caldwell Airport east of Morristown, but too much of the time would be spent doing their paperwork. Having already done that sort of VA (Veterans Administration) paperwork for returning vets for Kentucky Flying Service, I knew that was not what I wanted to do. Plus, as a part-time job it wouldn't generate enough income which meant finding another part-time job and hoping that the two of them together would make the effort worthwhile.

Then I heard that a fairly new business at Lincoln Park Airport not too far from home, just east on I-80, was ready to hire a sales manager. Bingo! Before I went to meet with the rather young Airport Manager, and then the money man behind him, I put quite a bit of effort into the resumé that I submitted for their consideration.

They already had quite a few CFIs (Certified Flight Instructors) and a working maintenance hangar. In addition to the Cessna franchise they'd just acquired, they were now trying for Piper. As I already knew the local Cessna and Piper people, I felt sure I would receive a good recommendation. I was grateful for whatever it was that helped them overcome any hesitancy about hiring a female sales manager. I had always tried to keep good relations with everyone I had met in aviation, so I never hesitated to network or ask for recommendations. There was only one person, I hoped never to see again – and he'd already been banished from the Cessna Zone scene.

Now that Jack had finished rebuilding '619's engine, I loved to start her up and hear her roar. She had a brand new, even more throaty rumble that made everyone turn around and look. She was all she had been before and now so much more. I knew Jack had paid a great deal of attention to the specs for racing and that I would never have to worry if the engine was torn down after a race win, because I knew it would be perfect.

He had been extremely careful with all the parts but especially the cylinders, and I could feel there was a bit more power than I had felt on previous races, yet she was as legal as she could be. I could not wait for the next race, but at that point I had no idea of when it would be. I swear '619 was chomping at the bit too, and each time we took off she rose so gracefully, but so fast from the tarmac, that it was really hard to call it quits when it was time to come back to earth.

I suppose we did a lot of pretending to be racing, '619 and I. We never reduced power in the air, but sadly when we were returning to base, the power had to be reduced, and there were no high-speed, low passes there before landing. I really missed that, and knew she did too. But I loved the fact that she was better than new, and I hoped it wouldn't be too long before that really fun HS LP (high speed low pass) could happen once more.

I found a press release that provided some solace for me, if not for her. We weren't the only ones who had problems with the commemorative air race. Many of the original batch of pilots didn't do so well, either. Only 75% of the racers in 1929 made it to the finish within the nine days of racing but that really is a spectacular fact in itself, considering the planes that they were flying: In addition to Amelia Earhart's Lockheed Vega, a forerunner of the Lockheed Electra that disappeared in later years somewhere over the

Pacific, there were Travelairs, DeHavilland Moths, Spartans, a Swallow, a Waco, a Rearwin, American and also Golden Eagles, Curtiss-Robins and a Mono-coupe. You won't encounter too many of any of them at the local airport anymore – you might try a muse-um, however!

I signed '619 up for a race the year following the calamity with the engine. Anxious to see how she per-formed in the next race, I enlisted Brooks to fly with me, but there were complications. My dear friend had a brush with death, as cancer in her left breast meant she had to go through a mastectomy and then radia-tion, all the while hoping it had not spread and noth-ing more remained either unseen or unfound.

My heart was in pain so deep that I did not know quite what to do at the thought I might lose my friend, my fellow racer and the closest thing to a sister I had ever experienced. We had had so many laughs to-gether and shed almost as many tears through the

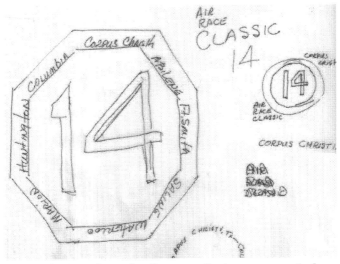

Designing the numbers for the race that was never to be.

short space of time we had been friends. What would I do without her at the other end of the phone. 'Light and love' was always her wish for me. She was Louisville's and my 'Angel Girl' and would be forever more.

Brooks and Kay

I put Laura's name in instead and we were accepted with the Racer number 14, but it was simply not to be, regardless. There was just one thing after another cropping up to keep us from going, and finally we threw in the towel and accepted the fact that we just weren't going to make it. So, there was no race for '619 but I continued to grow in my personal experience and love of the airplane, and that was truly a gift from her in teaching me how to go beyond my boundaries, my limitations. She was a prime example of that for me.

Chapter Nine

Shangri-La Grand Prix Air Race   Racer #2

The next winter a new race was formed and announced, named the Grand Prix, with the starting point being Shangri-La Airport, Oklahoma. It would also be the end of the race, as the course zig-zagged around Tyler, Burns Flat, Roswell to the west, and then headed east and south to San Angelo and Laredo. Heading back again to the east we would fly the timing lines at Waco, Monroe and then on to land back where we started. This turned out to be only 2098.49 miles, which was much shorter than most of our races except our previous one. That one was even shorter because we did not finish!

Route of the Shangri-la Grand Prix Air Race

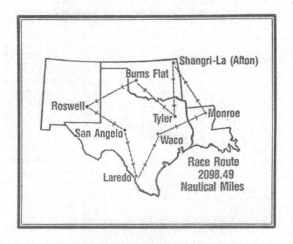

Designated Airports	Nautical Miles
Shangri-la Airport, Afton, Oklahoma	
Pounds Airport, Tyler, Texas	255.25
Clinton-Sherman Industrial Airpark, Burns Flat, Oklahoma	261.02
Roswell Industrial Air Center, Roswell, New Mexico	291.52
Mathis Airport, San Angelo, Texas	235.83
Laredo International Airport, Laredo, Texas	235.63
James Connally Airport, Waco, Texas	275.95
Monroe Municipal Airport, Monroe, Louisiana	261.74
Shangri-la Airport, Afton, Oklahoma	281.55
Total Route Milage	2098.49

The biggest thrill for me was that it was the first of that cross-country type and length of race that would allow men to participate. Paul had always been such a huge supporter of his girls going off and having the adventure of racing. He had been at many of the starts and all of the finishes of the ones that '619 and I had flown, and had even flown out to the Las Vegas start with Laura and me. We had been a bit 'heavy' on that trip and the plane had managed well, but even so, Paul had had quite a few pucker moments.

When I suggested he fly this one, he had accepted immediately, but then had major concerns that his flying wasn't up to the level I required for a race. Since I felt in this race that navigation and timing was actually more critical than the flying of the plane, I needed to have him fly because I knew he would measure up - eventually.

Paul Blevins contemplating flying his first air race.

Normal flights seldom have the precision needed to participate in a race. As a general rule, no one cares if it takes a minute or two longer to get where you're going if you are slightly off course. Auto pilots do a fairly decent job of it, but they are not set up to maintain the exactness of course and altitude needed for straight line flying when not using navigational aids. With the new instrumentation available now, you can choose waypoints that do a good job. However, at this time in 1981 a steady hand on the wheel, one that could hold a degree or half-degree heading correction, would get you there faster than your competition. The same applied to altitude. Wandering all over the sky does not make for a good time on that leg!

As I recall, there were thirty-seven male pilots who signed on for the race including Paul. We drew #2 which was an uncomfortable sensation – way too close to our #1 position in the previous, unfinished race. Surely, we had had all the 'bad' luck we would ever have in that last race and now we should be totally done with it. Sure. Like there is a giant scoreboard somewhere that makes sure the odds stay even. Although I do believe we are never given more than we can handle, it seems that philosophy does not hold true all the time. Eventually, life does seem to work out though.

I am sure that so far in this story, it is evident that living in New Jersey was not exactly my cup of tea. After we had been there for six months, Paul and I had had a fairly loud and upsetting discussion about it.

In addition to my unhappiness, it seemed that he wasn't having the greatest time in his job, either. But this was where the job was, and if I couldn't manage to live with it, then he would quit and we would find somewhere else to live.

After all the years he had invested in General Motors, there was no sense in doing that. After all, originally he had been told we would only be in New Jersey for a year. Surely I could manage another six months, if he could. So I shut up about any and all of my displeasures.

Guess what? It was now four years later, and we were signed up and ready to pack '619 and head for

Oklahoma and the race start. I was standing at the Lincoln Park Airport flight ops desk talking to several of my customers when I got a call from Paul. He never called me at work unless it was something important or something that couldn't wait, so I was cautious when I answered.

He asked if I could take a minute, and I answered yes, nothing much was going on that I couldn't put on hold. Then he said he had been transferred to Charlotte, NC, and was heading for a meeting there. I was silent for more than a few moments and then asked, "Have you actually been transferred or are you just going for an interview for the job there?"

"No," he replied, "I have the job and will report there on April 1st to begin the job." That was the very next week.

"OK. Well then, let me just say something I have been waiting to tell you. New Jersey. The whole state. Sucks!" At this, heads whipped around in astonishment, both at my words and my tone. Well, I had waited three-and-a-half years to finally get my unhappiness off my chest! However, I had not really intended to have such a large or surprised audience.

I loved Charlotte. One time when we had driven by on the way home from seeing Laura in Atlanta I had looked at the buildings downtown and expressed my opinion (out loud) that Charlotte would be a nice place to live. Of course we were heading back to New Jersey and *anything* else sounded good. My impressions of the city came back and I found I was really excited at the idea that Charlotte would be our next home.

Then it hit me. If this was Friday and he would be

in Charlotte on Monday, what about the race? We had planned on leaving Wednesday for Oklahoma, since the race inspection and impound started Friday. Saturday had mandatory pilots' briefings, so even if I flew out there alone, he would have to be there for that. The race started the following Monday.

But for once, Paul had added the race to the equation of the timing of our move. He would meet me at the race start, but at the end of the race we would fly together to Charlotte rather than going 'home' to NJ, and I would look at houses. I only had sixty days to complete the move and since moving to New Jersey had been such a fiasco from day one, we needed to choose a house quickly and get things rolling as fast as possible. I wanted out of New Jersey. Jack was the one thing I had found that was good in New Jersey. He and his wife, Dot, had turned out to be very, very good friends.

I had found success as sales manager at Lincoln Park, so that part of leaving would be sad for me too. At the beginning, the young airport manager questioned much of what I did. Even though many times I acted on instinct, I understood his need for information and willingly explained (when I could) what I was attempting to do. On other occasions, I just had to do it, then try to explain later.

As an example, early on, I had seen a pretty rough-looking character wandering around amongst the planes tied down at the far end. The boss was going to send one of the line-boys down to move him out, but I had a hunch. Yes, he had worn-out jeans and a cowboy hat that had been through the wars somewhere, and his shirt was sun-bleached and very thin, but when I walked down the line to come close enough to greet him, there was a twinkle in his eye. He was sunburned and spare, like a wind might have blown him in. He nodded to my hello, how are you, and waited to see what I would do. I did nothing, but leaned against the plane he had been sort of looking at. I say sort of because he was trying not to display much interest.

"Lovely day for around these parts," I said. "You don't look like you are from around here."

He said, "You the sheriff in town?"

I answered, "Just might be." And grinned.

"No, I am from Florida," he said.

I said my folks lived down in Lehigh Acres, did he know it?

"Reckon they be old folks", this coming from one who was not a youngster himself.

He asked what year the plane was that we were leaning against and I told him. Then he asked if I knew of any planes for sale. Yes, so happened I did. And so the dance started. We wandered around a bit more, I answered non-questions and then he said he had better be going.

My boss was having a fit when I walked back into the office. "What did he want, what was he doing out there?"

I answered, "He didn't rightly say, yet."

Boss said, "Well, don't spend any more time on the likes of him."

The next morning he was back. I made my way down the tie- down line and greeted him.

"Name's Charlie," he said.

"Mine's Kay, but don't hold it against me."

When he chuckled I knew we could get down to business. Soon I was pulling aircraft logs from the files and we were climbing in and out of all the older single engine aircraft I knew were for sale. We spent all morning ambling about, but I was very careful not to give a sales pitch. Of course, I would offer any details I knew about each plane, but nothing that might indicate why one plane was better than another. He began to ask more pointed questions that told me he definitely knew more than he was saying about airplanes, their parts and their value.

He left again as he had the day before and I heard the same grumbling from the boss about the time wasted on the old man. Yet I still had a hunch, and as I was handling all the other clients, too, without any problem, I could not see any harm in my waiting game with Charlie. Funny, this was the second Charlie I had connected with recently, but this one was still a bit of an unknown quantity.

On the third day Charlie came in and said, "Time's come to do a little business." And so we did.

When I walked into the office with a check for five airplanes, the boss still grumbled, the check might not be good. I suggested he have the bank verify it because the planes were leaving for Charlie's flight school the following morning. Seems he lost some planes in a storm and had been looking for replacements when he came wandering into our place. The planes did not belong to my boss, but he would get a healthy cut before the money was distributed to the owners. I had made a lot of people very happy. Pretty soon the boss left me to do the job I loved without any interference.

As my part of the business grew, so did my reputation for fair dealing. Sometimes in order to sell a new Cessna or Piper I had to sell the buyer's current plane to make the deal. And sometimes I had to sell the next buyer's plane to finish that deal. This all meant there was a lot of financial paper crossing my desk and one day I got a phone call from a manager of one of the NY banks that handled much of the aircraft sales financing in the region. He thought K Blevins was a man. Can you beat that!? But he still said he wanted to meet me. Would I have time for lunch?

I am always interested in why people do things. We had a lovely lunch, but the man waited until the end when we were having our coffee to explain why he wanted to meet me. He would hire me if he could, yes, but he didn't think I was interested in the banking end of aircraft financing. What he really wanted to know was how I was doing it. "Doing what?" I asked.

"Selling so damn many planes!" Since I didn't have a sales staff, he figured someone really good must have trained me or was helping me. And what was my secret?

He said I was outselling everyone in the tri-state area, and now he found out I was doing it by myself and he had to know how.

I took my time in formulating my answer. "Well, my boss won't let me take anything into inventory, and he has no floor plan to speak of, so I have to sell it before it gets here and frequently sell the trade-in before it gets here too, so it means a lot of planes move on through." But secretly, I was delighted that he thought it important enough to come all the way out here to ask me. Did it make any real difference in anything? Nope, but it was nice.

After Paul's call to me about moving to Charlotte, NC, I went in and told the boss I would clean up all the deals that were pending, but that when I left for the air race in just a few days I would not be returning there again to work. He had heard about my comments on the phone at the desk and was gracious enough to say he hoped I liked North Carolina. He said it as if I was moving to the sticks but I let it go. No point in saying that my heart was singing even if he thought it was a hick place to be.

# # #

I packed and made my way west to Oklahoma. I had never started a race that far east before so it was a bit strange to get to the start so quickly from my home base. Paul did arrive without mishap and while we spent most of any free time talking over details of the move, we were able to spend enough time on the race route, so that I felt good about it all. I was truly looking forward to the move and Paul said he had really enjoyed his introduction to the new Zone. He did think he would find it a much slower pace than he was accustomed to, but decided he would quickly get the hang of it. My first question was, "Where are the airports?"

Almost too soon the race began. On the first leg of the race, I gave Paul the course heading and altitudes to which he would need to adhere, as all that information had been decided after our last weather briefing. I watched carefully for wind drift and any changes. Suddenly, I realized we were off course and I reminded Paul of the heading. Thinking the wind must not be as forecast, I gave Paul a correction of half of a degree, and he said something like, "You have got to be kidding!"

Well, no, I wasn't. He did not think he could hold it that closely, but I kept giving him the impossible changes, and somewhere about the third leg of the race he was doing a much better job of it. He was beginning to find that my directions were not so impossible after all, but it *was* damned hard work.

I believe the most fun of the whole trip for Paul was on our way to Laredo from Roswell. We were contending with headwinds at the altitude we had chosen, so I kept giving him lower and lower altitudes. It was harder for me to see the checkpoints off in the distance while we were so close to the ground, but I was watching our times and knew that was what we had to do.

Thankfully there were few people, or habitations we'd need to avoid, but there were cows and sheep. When they heard '619 roaring too close in on them they would all rush headlong into whatever cover there might be. Sometimes it was only a massive bush, but there would be twenty to thirty animals rushing under it for cover.

The thought of all them crashing together in the middle tickled him way too much, and the tears of laughter mingled with the beads of sweat from the hot Texas sun and almost blinded him. That is not so good when you need to see low-hanging wires or flimsy skeleton like towers in order to avoid them. But the laughter still echoes in my memory.

Cattle making a mad dash for cover from the sound of the engine.

The best part of it all for me was hearing the voice of '619 roar once again. And we were flying at full speed across the timing lines in that high-speed, low-pass configuration I had missed so much. I was right, too, in that she felt more powerful than ever before, and I was ecstatic with her performance. I felt no vibration in my feet, only the feeling of a smooth running engine.

And from the first leg I watched our performance compared to what I had estimated and it was happily much faster than expected. We were on course to win this race! Now that Paul held course better than he had ever known he could, we stayed right on the money as far as the fastest line to fly.

He was experiencing the cushion of air, called 'ground effect' that is found when flying just a few feet above the ground, touching the yoke slightly to lift up and float over wires and obstacles in our path and then settling lightly back down into that lovely cushion. Ground speed while in ground effect was as much as five miles an hour faster than just twenty feet higher, but it took extreme concentration and Paul was learning why we had always been so wrung out when we finished a race.

Our luck seemed to run out as we swung northeast to Waco from Laredo. A huge storm was becoming a deciding factor for all the racers. When you are navigating between storm cells and their possible accompanying fog and lowered visibility, it is easy to lose track of your course, but I was working hard at intuiting which way was best around each obstacle or cell.

All these races were VFR, or Visual Flight Rules, which means, generally speaking, you need three miles of visibility, and clear of clouds, which was becoming more difficult by the mile. We had a hard time finding Waco but finally found a radio tower that said "WACO" and I knew that to be to the southwest of the outskirts of Waco.

The tower was mostly obscured, except at the very lowest two hundred feet of the red and white bands marking it. The airport was pretty much north of town but we finally found it and crossed the timing line more tentatively than usual, so that we could circle back to land without getting in the heavy precipitation and fog again.

There were still a few racers like us checking weather and trying to figure out how to get to Monroe, LA, in the glop, and there were a lot of pilots just walking up and down the tie-down area trying to see through the mists, hoping to see if a good opening should occur through the weather systems. No one could say anything for sure about the best scenario. Some eventually got tired of waiting for anything sure and just took off. Most returned.

I would have liked to put one more leg behind us because the next day meant we had to make it to the end of the race at Shangri-La. If the weather had been beautiful I would have said no problem but we were forecast to have more of the low visibility crap and we might get stuck like we had in Waco. A good night's sleep did seem to be the best option, though, for safety.

The next morning after waiting a while for an opening, I decided we needed to try as time was running out. We flew the timing line after taking off to restart our clock, and immediately went into the sketchy visibility with lots of moisture hanging in the air. Once in a while it seemed to be pretty good as we traveled east and then it would close down on us, but we made it without incident to Monroe. Only one more leg to go. The cockpit was a bit like a sauna as nothing ever dried out in this warm front through which we were navigating.

As we passed Hot Springs, I commented that it was our default if we couldn't get through, hoping against hope that would not be the case. There is a very gradual rise in elevation as you fly from the Hot

Springs area to that of Fort Smith. Paul was having a difficult time distinguishing where the moisture was thinnest while maintaining three-mile straight-ahead visibility, and suddenly neither of us could determine for sure what was ahead or which direction to turn – right or left – for better vision.

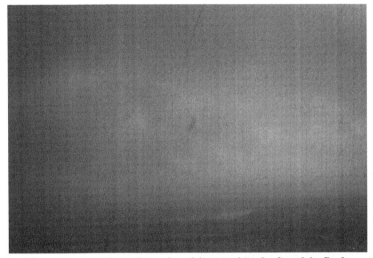

You can see the plane banking to land after his fly by.

First you see him and then you don't!

Keeping track of the other racers – not easy.

Getting an internal nudge I said with a sharp voice, "Make a 180 (degrees) NOW!" And bless him he instantly made a tight turn and we roared back into the slightly better visibility. I might not have made it clear before, but during all of this low-level flying in this glop, we had been flying mostly at 155 MPH, so if you hesitate even a tiny bit, you are apt to, very rapidly, find yourself in trouble.

We went back to Hot Springs and landed. We heard that some pilots with faster planes had made it through before it closed down, but until something changed we were stuck. I was to learn when I got home that Don Flowers, one of Cessna's insurance guys who was a pretty good friend, had also been trying to get through the same area about the same time that we had tried and turned back. He had not been in the race but just happened to be flying in the same area.

Unfortunately, Don had run smack into the same deceptive ascending terrain and died on impact. That was always the risk. We were the lucky ones. It was obvious that we would not have recognized the marginal change either. So, was it '619 that told me to turn back? Something definitely did and being so connected to her, I can believe she had a big part in it. That may be a bit much for some folks to agree with, but I believe it, so there it is.

Each moment we were on the ground, I anxiously watched the weather prognosis for the tiniest chance to get through to Oklahoma. I was also watching my watch as I knew exactly when the go/no go moment was and finally I said, "Let's do it." As we left, many of the others waiting there for the weather, also decided it was the last chance, and took off behind us.

It wasn't good. Paul still had to weave in and out of pockets of really poor visibility and rain cells, and we could not fly the direct course but we could stay close enough to it that I was able to keep track of our position, and I still thought we had a chance. The rules of the race were that you must finish (fly the timing line) by published sunset or be disqualified. We were either just going to make it or just going to miss it.

In spite of all the weather problems, I knew we had a superb time on all our legs except this last one, but even with that I felt we had a real chance to win. The tears started rolling down my cheeks when we were only minutes out from flying the timing line. Paul was still working hard to get us there and fly the timing line without mishap. As exhausted as he was, he did not want to make any mistakes in the final phase. I kept looking at my watch and the tears kept coming.

We had missed it. According to my watch we had missed sunset by 16 minutes, yet the sun was still partially visible to us. Paul was not aware that I was crying until we were actually directed to our tie-down. Instead of smiling congratulations, I was totally tear-stained and sat with my head bowed. We had done so well, but we had missed it in spite of all our best efforts. I wiped my face and we got out to greet the rest who had landed before we did. There were still quite a few behind us, and all were glad to be done finally.

But yes, indeed, we had missed it. There was no solace in the fact that after handicaps were taken into account, we had posted the best time over all, and if we had made it before published sunset we would have won. Even with the last leg, and the time spent in Hot Springs, we had the best time.

That fact pleased me but I knew it didn't matter. Rules are rules. It didn't matter that we had obeyed them when others were definitely fudging the VFR rules. But we knew we'd done our best, actually staying within them to the very best of our abilities.

If we had been fudging at the area around Fort Smith and had gone solely on instruments to get through the area, my thought is that we might have sealed our own fate. Especially down low under the indeterminate cloud decks where the only VFR was to be found. I am quite sure some had said to heck with it and ascended and went by instruments, but that is not playing the game, and I felt there is no real satisfaction in that. We did have the gratification of having flown the best time, but there always was a tinge of sadness to it.

Paul and '619 in her new hangar at Wilgrove Airport

The four pilots of N80619: Kay, Laura, Brooks and Paul

Chapter 10

I found I could not bring myself to stay around for the banquet, and Paul really did have to get back to his new job, so the next morning we took off and headed to Charlotte. We landed at the large Charlotte airport although it wouldn't be our home airport, but the next day I returned to New Jersey to get a real estate agent working on the sale there, and also to start the process of winnowing out our belongings.

We were to have a yard sale, and fortunately our son and his new wife were there to help with that. But in between agents and sorting I decided to take my final walk in the woods near home to say goodbye to the area where I used to go to get my mental attitude adjusted.

There were still piles of leaves from winter that had blown across the path and crunched under my feet, but suddenly my foot went deeper and the crunch was not the leaves but a bone in my left ankle. New Jersey had smote me one last time!! The leaves had covered a hole just waiting for my foot to find it.

I was in Mt. Arlington, about a mile from the car. I was still driving the Corvette, which had a stick shift. The only medical help was downhill. I could see no help anywhere around me, so, limping with the help of a branch, I made my way out of the woods and to the car. Once in the car, I managed to depress the clutch enough to start and then coasted much of the way down to the doctor's office in first gear. After the x-ray, the doctor wanted to know who was with me and when I said I had driven myself, he asked where from.

When I told him, he looked at me strangely and said that it would be easier going home as there would be a cast on that leg, but it would be better if someone could come and help. No one could. Everyone would hear about it at a much later date. New Jersey, you won, all of it, you won. I was NOT getting out in one piece but I was definitely getting out. Finally.

# # #

My next trip to Charlotte was by commercial airline. Paul met me and we had lunch with the real estate agent who said upon meeting me that most likely I would want to see only ranch or one-level homes since walking was an issue. I liked her immediately! And finding a house was not at all difficult, so very soon we had signed the necessary papers. But my main itch was to see the airport that Paul thought would suit '619 – and us – the best.

Forget houses! Airports were what rang my bell! That's what would get my baby down here with me once again, so that was what was important. We settled on a small airport called Wilgrove. No, it did not have a restaurant or many of the amenities we had in NJ but the fact it wasn't NJ was enough. We wouldn't be living as close to it as I would have liked, but in time we would build our retirement home much nearer to the airport. Not that we were able to retire there though! No, even though Paul had been told we would retire in Charlotte and not be moved again. Sure. And we even believed it. Then.

The move from New Jersey was accomplished within the allotted sixty days, and '619 was flown down and housed under a carport type hangar at a small rural type airport named Wilgrove. She really stood out from all the rest with all her race regalia and stars. It was a small strip but it had gas and she could slumber peacefully until we finished with all the moving stuff. After all, there would be no races until the next year so there was time.

And of course once we were reasonably settled in, I began my search to look for ways to support the costs of '619. I happened upon a listing for a sales rep position. It seemed I met all the qualifications listed, so I applied. It wasn't long before I was invited for an interview. Nothing indicated what kind of interview it would be, but I quickly discovered that it was to be a group interview.

When I walked in, I found a board room with a huge long table surrounded by chairs all around, many of which already had very professional looking men seated in them. The table eventually filled and, as usual, I was the only woman. That was pretty much the norm for me; therefore it was all OK.

Then the interviewer explained that we each had to 'sell' the rest on why we should be chosen for the position. He had given us some information about Spartan School of Aeronautics in Tulsa, OK, and with that he turned it over to the first candidate. Many of the applicants went on and on about their many talents, skills and abilities, and some said not much at all. I like to think I was somewhere in the middle, but I do remember having said something at the end – that even though I knew how qualified they all must be, yet I was certain I was the best 'man' for the job.

That brought a laugh, as many had acknowledged me being the 'the lady in with the gentlemen'. I was certain that this position would be a really good fit for me. It would mean travelling all over the state of North Carolina interviewing mostly young people who wanted a career in aviation, and I knew it was something I would enjoy. It also meant I could earn as much as I desired, while choosing my own work schedule and without having to follow anyone else's constant direction.

Later when the trainer asked me in for a second interview, it was really only to tell me that the job was mine, and that he was totally impressed by my speech. Although I could not then remember much of what I had said, I had known that the position would be perfect for me, and apparently that had come across loud and clear. I was flown out to Tulsa to learn about Spartan School, and then off I went to the small cities and towns where there were young people, most of whom wanted an opportunity, but also had an interest in aviation, resided. Some just wanted to get out of the small town they lived in. I understood both reasons very well.

I was fortunate to have made the list of the top sellers from the very beginning. My checks went to pay for the upkeep of '619, and by the time we had been in Charlotte for only a short while, the mortgage on '619 was paid off. Even so, hangar fees, gas and maintenance still required some effort on my part.

But then as so often happens, life gets in the way.

# # #

Agnes was Paul's mother. She was the very picture of an Italian mother, with a beaming smile, a twinkle in her eye, and a fairly large huggable bosom over which she normally folded her hands and arms. I first met her at Selfridge AFB in 1954 when her son introduced me to her after a CAP encampment. She exuded love. I treasured her from that day, letting her be the warm and caring mother I felt loved me more than my own mother had. I always knew she loved me. Whatever I might have done or would do, it would not have mattered to her, the love was there and always would be.

One day early in 1982, Agnes called and asked if she could come to Charlotte for a short visit. She knew she was always welcome for any length visit, so we naturally wondered why she'd asked. It seemed she had bone marrow cancer, and her prognosis was not good. She wanted to know if she could hospice with us. She did not want to spend her last days in Michigan, alone or at least not without us, so could she come to stay? Of course the answer was yes. Charlotte was a wonderful place for her to come to.

Even when we lived in Michigan during our various transfers there, and were handy to help her, I was the one who washed her feet and took her to the doctor or hospital, for her various problems: whether it was a stroke, shingles or medicinal side effects. It just seemed natural that I would then be the one to administer her seventeen medications and learn to give her the required four daily shots. This meant keeping a chart with times and amounts figured out and notated, so she wouldn't get into trouble with her meds.

It would be so much easier at our house, where

the weather was pleasant and the bird song filled the air and we could have coffee on the deck out back in the sunshine. We all seemed to think laughter was an antidote for anything bad, and so we all laughed a lot.

She had married someone some years earlier who had promised to share fun times with her, and early on she did have some good times and it was all good. But he was not in it for the long haul, especially when it included caretaking. Oh, he was around sometimes, but mostly he was back in Michigan, which was OK with us. I could go on about the stories she told us and the secrets we shared during those months. Not having him around made that time so much easier.

Toward the end of her time with us, I began having difficulty breathing due to compression of my heart and lungs. Lifting Agnes at first, when she was about 230 pounds was difficult and as the months went by, it took a severe toll on my scoliosis. Even by the end, when she was down to 170 pounds, it was more than my body could handle.

Soon I was on traction and that old standby from flying '619, my oxygen tank, each night, and after finally getting an appointment with the best spine doctor in the area, I also had a metal brace to support me during the day for which I was extremely grateful. There was an agreement, too, for a standing surgery appointment for six weeks after Agnes died, whenever that should turn out to be. It seemed way too soon that I was able to keep that surgery appointment.

Agnes would have loved the end of the story after her death. She had asked rather than a funeral to have us gather dog wood blossoms, take champagne and rent a float boat to find the deepest fishing hole in

Lake Norman, where we were to scatter her ashes along with the dogwood blossoms while drinking a toast to love and long life.

As she died in January of 1983 we had to wait for spring and the dogwood blossoms, and during that time her husband called and insisted he wanted her ashes. Seems he had hooked up with Agnes's brother's widow and they had decided to bury her ashes alongside her brother. He did not care what Agnes's wishes were. Paul was in a real quandary over this.

When the dogwood trees were in blossom we did rent that float boat. And yes, we had a lovely ceremony with laughter in the sunshine while we spread the blossoms and ashes to float and then sink to the depths. A great send off! And we also had many chuckles about the $700 it cost to bury the fireplace ashes next to her brother. We were sure her brother would have laughed too.

# # #

Two surgeries later and being in a full body cast for eight months, I returned home after six weeks in the hospital to find life quite different. For one thing someone had moved all the light switches! The surgeries that had taken place and the stretching involved between the two of them had made me three inches taller. Nothing was as it had been. Paul had to grab me by the neck of the cast and just above my knees to lay me down for sleep. And get me up again. Someday I may write about all the rest of the fun things that we went through, but for now I just prefer not to think about it!

But while caring for Agnes, and then going

through the surgery and recuperation, I had not flown '619 at all, much less in a race. I had not even heard her voice. Paul had spent as many hours of the day as possible first with his mother and then taking care of me. So he had not had any time to fly, either. There was no one except Laura that I would have trusted to take her up, and so she waited, tucked into her hangar with the bright white stars on the brilliant blue of her cowl. All dressed up for the party and nowhere to go.

# # #

Thank goodness there were no more payments to be made on '619's purchase. The only real expenses for her were hangar fees, insurance and the required maintenance. Paul did take time to fly her up to Jack in NJ for her annual inspection, but that was also to keep him current according to the FAA regs, and to fill Jack in on our situation. Laura would have to recertify me when I finally got out of my cast, but I also had to pass an FAA medical examiner physical and that took a bit of doing, as it is unusual to have someone be taller than the time before.

Finally, though it was handled, but my surgeon said I could no longer train students because of the probable bouncing that a student might do. It would take three years for all the nerves to re-grow through the wide swath of back that had been filleted - twice. After I was out of the body cast I spent an additional year and half in a metal brace. But at least, I was able to visit '619 and pat and hug her, and once in a while even fly her with Laura – just to hear her voice and feel her respond to my touch.

The first time out of my body cast, when I was allowed to go see her, I approached from the rear. Since she had a high wing, I was totally surprised to bash my head on the rear section of the aileron. It drew blood which dripped down my forehead while I giggled. I had always been able to walk unobstructed under her wing, so it was another adjustment to being taller than I had been most of my life. Three inches is a huge adjustment!

The other weird thing was the first time Laura and I took '619 up, my perspective was skewed. After all the hours I had flown '619, I now had a totally different picture to assimilate now that I was three inches taller. I had to learn to land all over again! What had been ingrained for all those years suddenly had to be thrown out the window. Now how strange is that when you are in your late forties??

Our airport was sold at that point, and even in my brace I decided to tackle aircraft sales again for the new owners. Of course we were in the midst of building a house that we had designed, the one that was to be our retirement home, but why not spend the rest of my time at an airport again. Except for one tiny additional detail.

My parents who were living in Florida were not doing at all well, and at some point while I was caring for Agnes, I made a rash promise to my mother that I would care for her when I was no longer needed for Agnes. Of course I had to have surgery, and get out of the body cast first, but there it was, still looming large at me – the promise to have them come live with us and for me to take care of them. That was why we were building a house, and one we designed with a DMZ (de-militarized zone) in the middle, a bedroom suite on each end. Did I remember to say I never ever really got along all that well with my parents?

# # #

The house was barely finished when Laura and Tom took our "Bomba" truck (with the roll up door) down to Lehigh Acres, Florida. They would bring up as much as they could of my parents' belongings on that first trip. Then came the last trip, when they brought dad's Cadillac, plus my mother and father to North Carolina. Well, it did mean I would no longer have to make trips down to Florida to see how they were doing. Now I could see them every morning and even all of every day.

The DMZ (a supposedly safe zone between two opposing forces) helped some at night. However, because of dad's increasing Alzheimer's and his penchant to brandish guns, Paul put a dead bolt on our bedroom door. Any time we could find a gun, and there were many, we secreted it away and gave the stash to our neighbor.

Very soon, as in the first month or so, we had to order a hospital bed for my mother as she was dealing with a great deal of fluid in her heart and lungs. She also needed a commode, to reduce the risk of falling while on the short trip to the bathroom. As she was a Christian Scientist, it took a lot for me to get her into my internist who had assisted before and after my surgeries. I trusted him.

He was a very special man, caring, understanding and smart. He examined her and said her congestive heart failure was increasing rapidly and talked her into at least having the fluid drawn so she could breathe easier. The horse-sized needle they brought in and inserted into her back about had me on the floor, but he said they took out forty pounds of fluids. I couldn't watch, so I couldn't verify his claim.

He also said he felt she might not have much longer to live, and I should be prepared. Soon nurses were coming to our home regularly as she wasn't able to make the trip into the doctor's office as often as he would have liked. We were in a fulltime care situation and I was still in the metal brace, and not supposed to lift anything.

It is amazing how much you can do if you have an adjustable bed! Unlike Agnes, my mother had lost all her excess weight some years before with TOPS, so once the fluid was drained she only weighed about 115 pounds. But that was still a lot for my newly re-constructed back to handle.

All too soon, it was weeks, and then months, since I had seen my beloved '619, or even flown her. My days and nights were full, and then one day after the nurses left and they had talked to the doctor, he called and said he felt she would not live out the week. I was watching dad more closely too. He could usually be found puttering about the five acres of woods, trimming and gathering branches. But our awareness of his wandering mind meant we always had to be sure where he had gone, so he wouldn't become lost, too.

Then out of the blue, we received a call advising us that my brother in Michigan had committed sui-cide. He was my only sibling but it was obvious I could not leave my parents to go to the funeral. So, with my blessings, the rest of my family left me to watch my mother's last days. They planned to return as soon as possible for the next probable funeral.

Even if my dad would probably not be cognizant if told of his son's death, I thought my mother was alert enough to understand the information. But how do you tell someone who is herself so close to death, that her beloved son was dead?

Indeed, a very strange thing happened. I decided that she did need to know, especially as I had always felt he was the favored child. In his adult life, he became a high school principal and had truly made her proud all through his life. I wasn't even sure it would register on her struggling mind, but I really felt it was worth a try. And so, I told her.

It was as if a light switch had been thrown. Slowly my mother began to recover. The doctors were equally surprised and did not expect it to continue, but imperceptibly it did. Months later the doctor said she needed to walk again and a therapist was sent, although she left in tears as my mother refused to try. The doctor said he did not want me to be forever trying to lift her, so she needed to begin the actual road to recovery.

A different therapist was eventually sent and she prepared me, by saying that she was going in my mother's room and would shut the door. I was not to interfere regardless of noise or what I might hear. She promised she would not hurt my mother, but she would get past the refusal to try.

There was actual screaming by my mother, but not the kind as if she was hurt, but rather an angry lashing out at this stranger who was trying to make her walk again. This went on for a long while, but when the nurse came out, I could see into the room and my mother was actually sitting up without the bed's help. Wow. I would always wonder what had been said.

But whatever it was, I could see that each time the therapist came there was a little more progress. Soon I was able to convince mother to ride in the wheelchair out to the dining table. Then a walker arrived, and was put into action. She began to be a little more chipper each day, but she was also pushing my buttons a bit harder all the time.

Around this time, while I was still trying to sell enough airplanes to keep '619's expenses handled, the owners of the airport said they wanted to divest themselves of it. It had not been whatever they were looking for and they wanted out. What an interesting proposition it could be for us! I was fairly certain we could make a modest go of it. When I was selling planes, I had started having activities like cheese and wine parties for the local pilots, and formed a club that would help make it more fun. We'd also developed other activities to consolidate the aviation enthusiasts.

But when we described to my parents what we were considering, mother got very upset and that meant father, also. They both insisted that we couldn't do that. It seems our first duty was to consider their care, and an airport would mean time and money spent elsewhere. Surely we were not going to jeopardize their future on such a radical scheme! Didn't we know we would surely lose everything if we tried? That was perhaps hard to dispute, so I didn't even try. Now that she was not going to die, it was a different ballgame altogether.

The more she became physically able the more was required of me. She would say something like "I want to bake a cake." Except that she could not actually do it, so it really meant she would tell me what she wanted done. When the cake was done and frosted, by me, and served at dinner for desert, and then if I passed on my serving, she went into a hurt little girl pout, and said, "I wanted to show I love you."

My refusal was a refusal of her love, and so the crazy-making continued, day in and day out. I realize she was still very ill, but there was a question in my mind about how long my body could continue to handle all the stress, as I was still healing from the deaths of Agnes and my brother, plus my own surgeries and still being in a metal brace.

The worst days of all came when all my hard-won credentials – my flight instructor, my commercial, and my instrument rating – all of them became useless pieces of paper. I had not been able to get to the mandatory FAA weekends and tests to update my knowledge of current rules and regulations. Like a teacher's CEU credits they must be handled during a specified time or your licenses become invalid. I watched mine slip by one by one as I cared for my two parents. Looking back should I, would I, could I have done anything different considering the equation? No, I think not. But I do wonder once in awhile, anyway.

# # #

My thoughts of '619 always brought me to the verge of tears. It was becoming obvious that I was not

175

going to be released to ever fly another race or live the life of a pilot, spending time at my airport again. Plus, it was not right that '619 was not being flown. Paul and I sadly agreed that it was time to find her a new pilot and life at a new airport. She had served me so well she deserved more than just sitting there, gathering dust and letting the mice nibble at her.

So I made my last aircraft sale. I was rather glad she was going up to the northeast part of the country. Better not to hear that tell-tale throaty growl, or see the white and blue plane with the accents of red, crossing my sky. And the stars. I wouldn't be able to see the stars on the cowl without tears welling up. No, it would be better for her to be far away from me.

I know Paul and Laura were just as sad, but '619 took a huge chunk of my heart with her when for the last time she lifted into the air, the pilot pulling the power back to normal cruise. However could she stand it not to fly full throttle from then on? And off to the north she flew, climbing steadily until she was out of sight and the last vestige of sound gone. I think the sky dimmed just a little. And the whole of my life along with it.

Epilogue

Last year my daughter walked in the door and said, "Guess what I found?" On a whim she had gone on the internet to see if she could discover anything about '619. What she found surprised the heck out of us. Indeed, '619 was still flying and Laura had the name of the person who owned her, so I grabbed the info and started backtracking to see just where she was now, because the name was not that of the person who had bought her from me all those years ago.

Soon I found a website of a small flying club, and there she was, pictured in landing configuration ready to touch down just a few feet from the runway. I thought my heart would break with the joy of seeing her, looking fresh and clean, and what was most amazing of all was her bright blue cowl. The stars were still emblazoned there! They still looked crisp and clean and bright as if they were part of the paint, which I knew was not so.

I was so very happy. Gathering up a picture of her in the last Powder Puff Derby with race number and all, and of course Laura and me too, I wrote a letter telling her new owner a bit about '619's racing history and just how exceptional we had found her to be, and sent it to the current owner's name, in care of the airport office.

For a very long time we heard nothing at all in response to my mailed packet. Then one day out of the blue there was a phone call. The man on the other end was so excited it took me a bit to understand what he was asking. Yes, I was Kay, and had owned N80619, and..............

Will wonders never cease? I knew baby was loved and she was happily training new pilots. We had both survived to live another day. In fact many days. What more could anyone ask? It all made life seem a whole lot better and I will always be grateful for all we shared.

Fly well, '619, and keep on, keeping on.

Dear Kay –

Hearing the sound of NOT RAW, but CON-
TROLLED and DIRECTED power from those Allison,
Pratt & Whitney,Rolls Royce & so many other fighter
aircraft engines of the WWII period just makes my
heart pound with awe at the engineering feats that
created them. Many air shows featuring WWII aircraft
have stirred my sense of pride that our own dedicated
assembly line workers in aircraft plants, during the
toughest imaginable economic times, were able to
craft those awesome machines that, in the end, de-
feated the powerful enemies sworn to defeat the US.
From my own passive experience I know that the
sound of Kay's plane's engine responding to her skill-
ful guidance will be with her for the rest of her life. A
final note: Kay was a classmate of mine and became a
friend in our senior year in high school. I was in awe
of her already having achieved certification in the
Civil Air Patrol and having run rescue missions to lo-
cate missing hikers, downed aircraft and such. I was
so pleased to learn just a few years ago via email con-
tacts with Kay that she had continued to pursue her
passion.

Sincerely offered,

John Martin, Class of 1954, Highland Park, Michigan,
Now living in Wells, Maine.

About the author –

This is the first book from Kay Blevins – but definitely not the last! Born in Michigan, she has since lived in several states, mostly east of the Mississippi River. In addition to her adventures detailed in this book, she has also been happily married to Paul for 58 years, and they have 2 children and 1 grandchild.

Kay spent 35 years in aviation as an instrument commercial pilot, CFI, selling aircraft (and cars), teaching, airport management, air race competitor; 15 years working as a sandblast designer in wood and glass, with 4 business locations, and 14 years caring for 3 aging parents before hospice care.

Obviously, some of these were done simultaneously – she's not really *that* old!

If you would like to contact Kay, her website is: www.kayblevins.com or you may reach her at Kayblevins1@gmail.com

WITHDRAWN

29491786R00105

Made in the USA
Lexington, KY
28 January 2014